East Anglia Edition
researched by Moira Biggs an[d]

Contents

Map	2
Free Places	3
Directory of Activities & Information	13
Boat & Train Trips	26
London	29
Historic Sites, Castles, Museums & Science Centres	45
Farms, Wildlife & Nature Parks	57
Theme Parks & Play Parks	67
Places to Go Outside the Area	71
Index	72

B3 Map References - refer to map on page 2 and locate the grid square to help you find out where everything is.

(A) Price code (defined in key on most pages) to help you budget your visits.

Schools School party facilities, visits by arrangement.

EH English Heritage Property

NT National Trust Property

Open
all year Winter opening too!

🎂✦ Birthday parties are organised where you see these signs.

A telephone number is given for most entries. Should you require special facilities for someone with a disability, please call before your visit to check suitability.

This publication is designed to provide accurate and appropriate information and we use best endeavours to ensure this. The accuracy and appropriateness cannot be guaranteed and such information may be changed without notice by the bodies concerned and information herein should therefore be used only as a guide and does not obviate the need to make appropriate enquiries of the bodies themselves. Published by Cube Publications. Printed by Southbourne Printing Co. Ltd. Artwork by Ted Evans Design. © 2002 Maureen Cuthbert and Suzanne Bennett. All rights reserved. No part of this publication may be reproduced by printing, photocopying or any other means, nor stored in a retrieval system without the express permission of the publisher.

You have helped Great Ormond Street Hospital Children's Charity this year marking 150 years of caring for sick children.

Great Ormond Street was opened on 14th February 1852 with only 10 beds. This was at a time when a third of all children born in the UK did not reach adulthood. Today the Hospital treats over 100,000 young patients every year, many with life-threatening diseases or conditions.

Through the sale of these guides we will have raised £18,000 since 1998. This year money raised by Cube will go towards Syringe Pumps. These pumps are necessary for safe and accurate administration of drugs to the patient.

We are proud to announce that a 6 pence contribution to the above charity will be made for each "Let's Go with the Children" book sold this season. Thank you for your support.

Registered Charity No. 235825 © 1989 GOSHCC

Published by
Cube Publications, 290 Lymington Road,
Highcliffe, Christchurch, Dorset BH23 5ET
Phone 01425 279001 Fax 01425 279002
www.cubepublications.co.uk
Email: enquiries@cubepublications.co.uk
2nd Edition
ISBN 1 903594 13 8

Let's Go with the Children guides are pleased to be in association with Renault and to be featuring the Renault Scenic multi-activity car.

MAP

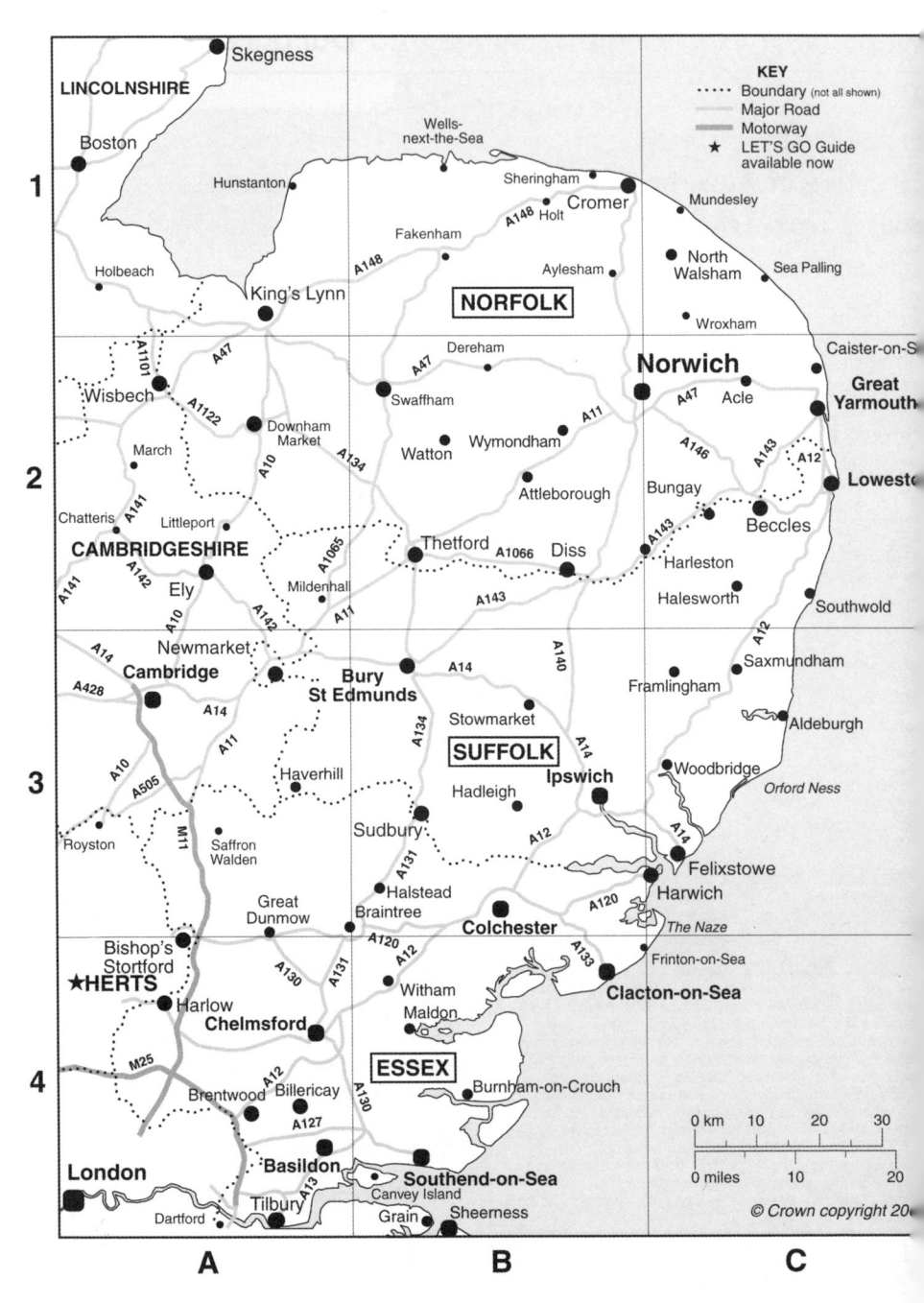

Ordnance Survey

KEY
- ····· Boundary (not all shown)
- —— Major Road
- ▬▬ Motorway
- ★ LET'S GO Guide available now

Free Places

This chapter includes museums, a selection of parks, open spaces and other places that freely offer family entertainment and enjoyment. Although free admission, there may be some car parking charges, extra charges for schools and special activities, or requests for donations.

The country parks marked (ERS) are owned and managed by Essex County Council Rangers Service. They offer a great day out with the children with plenty to explore. There are wonderful educational opportunities for school parties and many school holiday activities. There may be a small car parking charge on Suns & Bank Hols in Summer at some sites. 01245 492211. (See Advert outside back cover.)

Award-winning Beaches

Norfolk, Suffolk and Essex are proud recipients of a clutch of seaside awards from the Tidy Britain Group's Seaside Award scheme. Meeting high standards of water quality and beach management, many of their beaches, both 'Resort' and 'Rural', have attracted high commendations. The 'Resort' beaches have good public access, facilities and activities on offer, while the 'Rural' beaches offer a quieter, more scenic environment. Listed below are the local award-winning beaches.

Essex Rural: Brightlingsea. **Resort:** Dovercourt, Leigh-on-Sea (Bell Wharf), Southend, (Shoebury Common, Shoeburyness East, Three Shells).
Norfolk Rural: Heacham (North & South), Sea Palling, Snettisham. **Resort:** Cromer, Great Yarmouth (Central and Gorleston), Hunstanton, Mundesley, Sheringham.
Suffolk Rural: Aldeburgh, Felixstowe (The Dip), Kessingland, Lowestoft (Gunton), Sizewell, Southwold (The Denes); Thorpeness. **Resort:** Felixstowe (South), Lowestoft (South & Victoria), Southwold (Pier).

A1 Schools / Open all year **Caithness Crystal,** 8-12 Paxman Road, Hardwick Industrial Estate, **King's Lynn.** See how this world-famous glass is made. There is an audio-visual area and factory shop with giftware and glass animals. Open daily 9am-5pm, Sun, 10.15am-4.15pm; ring for times of glass-making. 01553 765111. www.caithnessglass.co.uk

Open all year **Norfolk Lavender,** Caley Mill, **Heacham,** off A149 between Hunstanton and King's Lynn. Visit the gardens and fields of lavender and herbs. There are guided tours from May to Sept; gift shops, tea rooms and a children's play area. Open daily 10am-6pm (5pm in Winter); closed 25th, 26th Dec, 1st Jan. 01485 570384. www.norfolk-lavender.co.uk

Open all year **Snettisham Coastal Park,** off A149 near **Snettisham.** Two waymarked circular walks pass through varied landscapes, from open grassland to dense reedbanks and open water. At low tide, the wide expanse of mudflats reveals a rich variety of wildlife.

Open all year **Titchwell Marsh,** RSPB, off A149 W of **Brancaster.** Each changing season offers new and wonderful delights among the freshwater reedbeds and lagoons, the saltmarshes and sand dunes of this picturesque coastline. There are nature trails, hides and a Visitor Information Centre. Special pond-dipping days and children's events during school holidays. Small car park charge. Open daily, Summer months, 10am-5pm, Sat-Sun, 9.30am-5.30pm; Winter months, 9am-4pm, Sat-Sun, 9.30am-4pm. Visitor Centre closed 25th, 26th Dec. 01485 210779.

13 **"The Backs",** Cambridge, provide a lovely walk for all ages to enjoy the ambience of the city with views of the Colleges across the river.

Open all year **Bridge End Gardens,** Saffron Walden is a tranquil oasis where time seems to have stood still. Explore the Dutch Garden and the rose garden and get lost in the Victorian hedge maze which has been restored and replanted to the original design. The maze and certain other parts of the garden may only be visited by appointment. Contact the Saffron Walden Tourist Information Centre for details. Open daily. 01799 510444.

Cambridge Colleges. Some of these famous seats of learning can be visited, although there are restrictions, particularly during examination time. Check with Tourist Information Office. 01223 322640.

Map Ref: Grid square on Page 2 Map   Schools: Facilities available   ● Birthday parties

MAP REFS		
A3	Schools Open all year	**Cambridge Darkroom Gallery,** Gwydir Street, for budding photographers, runs courses and workshops. Open Wed-Sun, 12-5pm. 01223 350533.
	Schools Open all year	**Fitzwilliam Museum,** Trumpington Street, **Cambridge,** houses an outstanding collection of paintings, antiquities, ceramics and beautiful artefacts from around the world. Guided tours Suns at 2.30pm. Open Tues-Sat, 10am-5pm, Sun, 2.15-5pm, some Bank Hols 10am-5pm. Closed 24th Dec-1st Jan, Good Fri & May Day Bank Hol. 01223 332900. Education Office 01223 332993. www.fitzmuseum.cam.ac.uk
	Schools Open all year	**Hinchingbrooke Country Park,** Brampton Road, **Huntingdon,** has 180 acres of open grassland, meadows, woodland and lakes with a wealth of wildlife. Whether walking the dog, exploring with the children or having a picnic everyone will enjoy the visit. Staffed Visitors Centre and a café at peak times. Educational activities, (phone for details and prices). Open daily. 01480 451568.
		Jesus Green, Cambridge, has acres of grass for play. In Summer there is a pool.
	Schools Open all year	**Kettles Yard,** Castle Street, **Cambridge,** houses a notable collection of 20th century paintings and sculpture. House open: Tues-Sun, 2-4pm, Gallery open: 11.30am-5pm. Closed Christmas and Good Fri. 01223 352124.
		King's College Chapel, Cambridge, has beautiful stained glass and a magnificent fan-vaulted ceiling. The public are welcome at some choral services during term time. 01223 331100/331212 for details.
	Schools Open all year	**Lammas Land,** Cambridge, has a playground and paddling pool. Occasional open air story-telling sessions in Summer.
		(For information on an extensive programme of Summer time children's activities in Cambridge city, call 01223 457521/457873.)
	Schools Open all year	**Sedgwick Museum of Geology,** Downing Street, **Cambridge,** has a magnificent collection of fossil animals and plants, rocks, minerals and gems collected worldwide. See hippopotami, wolves and bears - all found locally! Open Mon-Fri, 9am-5pm, closed 1-2pm. Sat 10am-1pm. Closed Christmas, Easter and Aug Bank Hol. 01223 333456. www.sedgwick.esc.com.ac.uk
		The Town Common, Saffron Walden, has a playground and an ancient turf maze which may not look much to adults, but is fascinating for children!
	Schools Open all year	**University Museum of Archaeology and Anthropology,** Downing Street, **Cambridge,** contains exhibits tracing mankind's development from the earliest times. The Anthropology Gallery exhibits culture from many regions of the world. Open Tues-Fri, Sats in Summer, 2-4.30pm. School parties by arrangement. Closed Easter and Christmas. 01223 333516. www.cumaa.arch.anth.cam.ac.uk
	Schools Open all year	**University Museum of Zoology,** Downing Street, **Cambridge,** has displays representing the rich variety of animal life. Exhibits include a reconstruction of a rocky shore, a killer whale and a giant spider crab. Open University terms, Mon-Fri, 2-4.45pm; University hols, 10am-1pm, 2-4.45pm. Closed Christmas and Bank Hols. 01223 336650. www.zoo.cam.ac.uk
		Wandlebury Park and Gog Magog Hills, 4 miles SE of **Cambridge** off A1307 has picnic site, walks and nature trail. Site of Iron Age Hill Fort. Good views and great for kite flying!
	Schools Open all year	**Whipple Museum of History of Science,** Free School Lane, **Cambridge.** This award-winning newly re-furbished museum shows a fascinating collection of scientific instruments. Opening times vary. Closed Christmas and Easter. 01223 330906. hps.cam.ac.uk/whipple.html
	Schools Open all year	**Wood Green Animal Shelters,** Godmanchester. There are lots of rescued animals to be seen including many that are unusual. Young supporters can join their own club. Look out for the wind turbine! Schools and birthday parties by prior arrangement. Open daily, 9am-3pm. Closed 25th-26th Dec. 01480 830014. www.woodgreen.org.uk

Map Ref: Grid square on Page 2 Map   Schools: Facilities available   ● Birthday parties

Free Places

A3 — Schools / Open all year — **Wood Green Animal Shelters,** Chishill Road, **Heydon**, near Royston. Visit all the rescued cats and dogs in their spacious runs. See also the other animals including lop-eared rabbits and guinea pigs. Young supporters can join their own club. Open daily, 9am-3pm. Closed 25th/26th Dec. 01763 838329. www.woodgreen.org.uk

A4 — Schools / Open all year — **Abbey Church,** Waltham Abbey. The Crypt Centre houses an exhibition about the town and Abbey. Open daily, 10am-6pm, 4pm in Winter. 01992 767897.

Schools / Open all year (ERS) — **Belhus Woods & Country Park,** Romford Road, **Aveley**, has a Visitors' Centre, refreshments, woodland and 3 lakes (2 of which offer fishing) providing a refuge for waterfowl. Open daily 8am-dusk. 01708 865628. www.essexcc.gov.uk/countryparks

Schools / Open all year — **Chelmsford Museum,** Oaklands Park, Moulsham Street, **Chelmsford**, houses a wide range of exhibits including an observation beehive. Visit the "Story of Chelmsford" display. The Essex Regiment Museum covers the period from the mid 18th century to the post war era. Open Mon-Sat, 10am-5pm; Sun, 2-5pm. Closed Good Fri, Christmas Day and Boxing Day. 01245 615100. www.chelmsfordbc.gov.uk/museums/index/shtml

Schools / Open all year — **Epping Forest District Museum,** Sun Street, **Waltham Abbey**, is a lively social history museum covering the Stone Age to modern times. Gallery of 19th century life features re-creation of Victorian shops. (Small charge for school parties.) Open Fri and Mon, 2-5pm, Sat, 10am-5pm, Tues, 12-5pm; May-Sept, Sun also, 2-5pm and other times by arrangement. 01992 716882. www.eppingforestdistrict.co.uk

Schools / Open all year — **Fairlop Waters Country Park,** near **Ilford**, consists of 480 acres of countryside with a 38 acre lake, where watersports can also be enjoyed.

Open all year — **Gloucester Park,** Basildon, is a 250 acre amenity close to the town centre, with fishing and boating facilities.

Schools / Open all year — **Hainault Forest Country Park,** Formal Area, **Chigwell Row**, is a designated country park. With its 4 acre fishing lake, rare breeds farm, orienteering course and a guided walks programme at weekends, the forest makes for a great day out. Visitor/interpretation centre. Open daily, 7.30am-dusk. 020 8500 7353.

Schools / Open all year — **Harlow Town Park,** off Second Avenue, **Harlow**, has 164 acres of scenic landscaped river walks, gardens and recreation. Attractions include Pet's Corner, an adventure playground and bandstand. Paddling pool open during School Summer hols. 01279 446404.

Schools / Open all year — **Hatfield Forest,** NT, just off the M11 at Jn 8, was once part of the Royal hunting forests of Essex. The forest is a Nature Reserve, there is a large fishing lake and an 18th century Shell House. Small car park charge. 01279 870678.

Open all year — **King Georges Playing Fields,** Ingrave Road, **Brentwood**, has a children's play area, crazy golf, picnic areas and open air splash pool in Summer.

Open all year — **Lake Meadows Recreation Ground,** Billericay, has a boating lake, putting, miniature golf, play facilities and petanque.

Schools / Open all year — **Langdon Hills Country Park,** between the A13 and Basildon town, consists of two areas, Westley Heights and One Tree Hill. Hikers and bikers can use the bridleways passing through farmland between the two. Ranger guided events throughout the year. Open daily 8am-dusk. 01268 542066.

Schools / Open all year — **Lee Valley Park Information Centre,** Waltham Abbey, located in the Abbey Gardens, provides information on local history and activities held in Lee Valley Park including an excellent schools programme. Open daily, Easter-Oct 9.30am-5pm; Nov-Easter, Tues-Sun, 10am-4pm. 01992 702200. www.leevalleypark.org.uk

Lee Valley Regional Park, stretches along 26 miles of the River Lee, from East London to Hertfordshire and offers a vast array of leisure and sporting activities. Take a picnic and explore the countryside, nature reserves and water areas. Details available from Lee Valley Park Information Centre at Waltham Abbey. 01992 702200.

Mill Meadows, Greens Farm Lane, **Billericay**. This 90 acre reserve contains fine examples of old grazing meadows and includes some rare species. 01268 550088.

Map Ref: Grid square on Page 2 Map   Schools: Facilities available   ● Birthday parties

MAP REFS

A4 Schools, Open all year — **National Motor Boat Museum,** Pitsea, is part of the Wat Tyler Country Park, and houses all manner of exciting power boats. Open Thurs-Mon, 10am-4.30pm, daily, School Summer hols. 01268 550077.

Noak Bridge, Eastfield Road, Noak Bridge. An area of mixed habitats covering 20 acres. There are several ponds and snakes and lizards are common. 01268 550088.

Open all year — **Norsey Wood,** Outwood Common Road, Billericay, is a 165 acre woodland with Ancient Monument status; it was the site of a massacre during the Peasants' Revolt in 1381, and has seen many archaeological discoveries. Open daily, 9am-dusk. 01277 624553.

Schools, Open all year — **Parndon Wood Nature Reserve,** Parndon Wood Road, Harlow, is a 52 acre sanctuary with two nature trails and observation hide. Open Suns, 9am-6pm (closed 1-2pm). Also Tues, 7-9pm, Apr-Oct. Group bookings, small charge. 01279 430005.

Queens Park Country Park, Rosebay Ave, Billericay. 60 acres of former parkland, now managed to enhance the area for wildlife. 01268 550088.

Schools, Open all year, (ERS) — **Thorndon Country Park,** Brentwood, accessed from The Avenue or Brentwood Road. The Visitors' Centre is jointly managed with Essex Wildlife Trust with interactive displays, refreshments and a gift shop. Approx. 500 acres of woodland, countryside and lakes to explore. Small car park charge Summer Suns & Bank Hols. Open daily 8am-dusk. 01277 211350. www.essexcc.gov.uk/countryparks

Schools, Open all year — **Thurrock Local History Museum,** Grays. A wide-ranging collection of imaginative displays covers the history of the area. There are many excellent historical reconstructions and an interesting programme of temporary exhibitions. Open Mon-Sat, 9am-5pm, closed Suns and Bank Hols. 01375 382555. www.thurrock-community.org.uk

Schools, Open all year — **Wat Tyler Country Park,** is just off the A13 near to Pitsea Station. The former Pitsea marshes have been developed to let the visitor enjoy an enormous range of countryside activities including a miniature railway. Open daily, 9am-dusk. 01268 550088.

Schools, Open all year, (ERS) — **Weald Country Park,** near Brentwood, has a barn Visitor Centre with landscape exhibition, gift shop and refreshments. The surrounding landscape includes picturesque open parkland suitable for picnics and games, an ancient deer park with large old trees, lake and meadow. Open daily 8am-dusk. Visitor Centre Apr-Oct, Tues-Sun, 10am-4.30pm, Nov-Mar, Sat & Sun 10am-4pm. 01277 216297. www.essexcc.gov.uk/countryparks

B1 Open all year — **Baconsthorpe Castle.** Well off the beaten track, this is the impressive ruin of a 15th century manor house. For sturdy walkers, an 8-mile circular walk through rural Norfolk takes in Holt Country Park where a leaflet is available from the Visitors' Centre. Open daily.

Schools, Open all year — **Blakeney Point,** NT. Access from Cley beach or by ferry from Morston and Blakeney. The 3 mile long sand and shingle spit is noted for its colonies of breeding terns and migrant birds. Grey and common seals can also be seen here, as well as a wide range of unusual seaside plants. Small charge for school parties. 01263 740241. www.nationaltrust.org.uk

Schools, Open all year — **Blickling Park,** NT, Blickling near Aylsham. A lakeside walk, a mausoleum cunningly disguised as a pyramid hidden away in the Great Wood - lots to explore and space to roam. Blickling Church has copies of 15th century brasses to rub. Open daily, dawn-dusk. 01263 738030. www.nationaltrust.org.uk

Schools, Open all year — **Brancaster Staithe,** NT, halfway between Wells and Hunstanton on A149 coast road. A huge area of salt marsh to explore. Weather permitting, a boat can be hired to visit English Nature's reserve on Scolt Head Island. (See also Brancaster Millennium Activity Centre in "Farms" chapter.) www.nationaltrust.org.uk

Schools — **Cromer Lifeboat & Museum,** The Pier and Gangway, Cromer. Cromer's dramatic sea rescue history is told here through models, pictures and photographs. The new Tyne-class lifeboat is on view at the lifeboat house. Open daily, Easter-31st Oct, 10am-4pm. 01263 511294.

Map Ref: Grid square on Page 2 Map   Schools: Facilities available   ● Birthday parties

MAP REFS

B1

Schools **Fakenham Museum of Gas and Local History,** Fakenham. On A1065
Open all year Swaffham Rd. A little chunk of history, this is the only complete (non-working) gas works in England. Learn how gas was made and how the men who made it lived. Open Thurs, May-Sept, 10.30am-3pm; Sept-Apr, closes 1pm. 01328 863150/855237/851696.

Schools **Foxley Wood,** NWT, off A1067 Norwich to Fakenham road. Believed to be over 6,000 years old, this is Norfolk's largest ancient woodland. Beautiful wildflowers in Spring. 01603 625540.

Schools **Holt Country Park,** off B1149, just S of Holt. Woodland and play area. Seasonal
Open all year events range from guided walks, pond-dipping, nightjarring, mountain bike adventure trails and shelter building/survival techniques. Visitor Centre open during school hols, 10am-4.30pm. Woodlands Officer, 01263 516062.

Open all year **Sheringham Park,** NT. Upper Sheringham. Viewing towers offer stunning views of the surrounding coast and countryside. Delightful waymarked walks and access to the North Norfolk Railway. Small charge for car park. Open daily, dawn to dusk. 01263 823778. www.nationaltrust.org.uk

Schools **Straw Museum,** Colby. A small-scale and unique collection of corn dollies and other straw work, plus intriguing examples of little known rural crafts. Small charge for parties. Open Easter to Oct, Sat and Wed, 11am-4pm. 01263 761615.

32

Schools **100th Bomb Group Memorial Museum,** Common Road, Dickleburgh. The original World War II control tower, now a museum, pays tribute to the men of the American 8th Air Force. Refreshments, shop, visitor centre and picnic area. Open Sat, Sun and Bank Hols, Feb-Oct, 10am-5pm; Wed, May-Sept, 10am-5pm; closed Nov-Jan. 01379 740708. www.100thbg.com

Bishop Bonner's Cottages Museum, Dereham. Teeny rooms in these three timber-framed early 16th century cottages house local exhibits. Open May-Sept, Tues, Thurs-Sat, 2.30-5.30pm. 01362 850293.

Schools **Brandon Country Park,** 1 mile S of Brandon on B1106, mostly wooded, has a Tree
Open all year and History Trail to follow, waymarked Forest walks and an Orienteering Course. There is a Victorian walled garden, a Visitors Centre and an adventure playground. Open daily, 10am-4pm, Oct-Mar; 10am-5pm, Apr-Sept (5.30pm weekends and Bank Hols.) 01842 810185. www.suffolkcc.gov.uk

Schools **Burston Strike School,** The Village Green, Burston. This building was erected to
Open all year house the scholars of the Strike School, famous for the longest strike in British history. Children's imagination will be sparked by the interpretative exhibition of schoolroom artefacts, documents and photographs. Key available during daylight hours; closed on national and local polling days. 01379 741565. www.burstonstrikeschool.org.uk

Open all year **Caister St Edmund,** near Norwich. The greenfield site of Venta Icenorum is Norfolk's forgotten town, once its capital. A marked circular walk with information boards takes about an hour.

Schools **International League for the Protection of Horses,** Overa House
Open all year Farm, Larling (off A11 between Norwich and Thetford). A recovery and rehabilitation centre for horses, ponies and donkeys, rescued from cruelty and neglect. Animal lovers can follow the information trail and visit the gift shop and café. Open Wed, weekends and Bank Hols, 11am-4pm. Closed Christmas. 01953 497219.

Schools **Knettishall Heath Country Park** can be accessed by various routes, one being
Open all year off the B1088 from Euston, S of Thetford. These 375 acres of heath, grassland and woodland provide a quiet place to enjoy walks on the waymarked trails and picnics and games in the open spaces. School and Information packs available. Open daily, 9am-dusk. Closed 25th-26th Dec. 01953 688265.

Free Places

Map Ref: Grid square on Page 2 Map   Schools: Facilities available   ● Birthday parties

MAP REFS

B2 Schools
Open all year
Ranworth Broad, NWT, off B1140 Norwich to Acle Road. The Broads Wildlife Centre is housed in a floating, thatched building, reached by way of a boardwalk through woodland, reedbeds and open water. Here, there are interactive displays and superb views over the Broad. An ideal family outing is completed with a boat trip across Ranworth Broad. Wildlife Centre open daily, Apr-Oct, 10am-5pm. 01603 270479. Schools, 01603 625540.

Schools
Open all year
Redgrave and Lopham Fen, Low Common, **South Lopham** near Diss. After 30 years of damaging water extraction the fens have been restored in an internationally celebrated project. The visitor centre has information about wildlife habitat and a shop and tearoom. Special events all year. Centre open Apr-Oct, Tues-Sun, 10am-5pm; Nov-Mar Sat & Sun 10am-4pm. 01379 688533. www.wildlifetrust.org.uk/suffolk/videx.htm

Schools
Open all year
Thetford Forest Park, Britain's largest lowland pine forest, is forestry at its best. Deep in the forest is High Lodge Forest Centre, which has information and displays about the forest, a shop and tea room. Waymarked walks, bike hire, play area, adventurous ropes course and Squirrel's Maze. A small car park charge. The Visitor Centre is open from Easter-end Oct 10am-5pm and from Nov-Easter, Sat & Sun 10am-4pm. 01842 810271.

B3 Schools
Open all year
Abberton Reservoir Visitor Centre, 6 miles SW of **Colchester** on B1026. A wetland of international importance for wildfowl. Flocks of swans, ducks and geese in Winter, terns and cormorants nest in Spring. The Centre has an observation room and five hides. Family Nature Days (weekends and school hols). Open daily except Mons, 9am-5pm. 01206 738172. www.essexwt.org.uk

Open all year
Abbey Gardens, Bury St Edmunds. In the grounds of the ruined Abbey are peaceful riverside gardens with putting, pets' corner and play equipment. You can also learn about the Abbey ruins. (See "Historic Sites" chapter.)

Schools
Open all year
Arger Fen Woodland, between **Bures** and **Nayland,** on the edge of the Stour Valley, has way-marked trails and a picnic area.

Open all year
Belle Vue Park, Sudbury, has a play area with swings and wooden adventure frame. There is also a pets' corner, aviary, putting, tennis and skateboard ramp.

Schools
Open all year
Bradfield Woods, Felsham Rd, **Bradfield St. George.** This National Nature Reserve is a beautiful ancient woodland, coppiced since the 13th century to harvest the timber in a sustainable way. Open daily. Visitor Centre open Sun afternoons and Bank Hol Mons. 01449 737996. Education Service 01394 380113. www.wildlifetrust.org.uk/suffolk/videx.htm

Open all year
Castle Park and Gardens, Colchester, has a boating lake, putting, crazy golf and a playground. You can also feed the ducks.

Clare Castle Country Park, is accessed off the A1092 from Clare. The Castle ruins and disused Railway Station make interesting centrepieces to wander around. Play area for younger children and a Visitor Centre. 01787 277491. www.suffolkcc.gov.uk

Schools
Open all year
Christchurch Mansion and Wolsey Art Gallery, Ipswich. The 16th century house in a lovely park has various furnished rooms and contains works by Gainsborough and Constable. The Wolsey Gallery holds workshops and children's holiday activities. Open Tues-Sat, 10am-5pm Summer, Sun, 2.30-4.30pm, (4pm in Winter). 01473 433554/433563. www.ipswich.gov.uk

Schools
Open all year
Dedham Art & Craft Centre and Toy Museum, High St, **Dedham,** has units on three floors. Crafts include resident artists, wood turning, candles and jewellery. There is a tea room and gift shop. Museum open Tues-Thurs, weekends and Bank Hol Mons 10am-5pm. Craft Centre open daily, 10am-5pm (closed Mons, Jan-Mar). 01206 322466.

Schools
Open all year
The Fingringhoe Centre, 5 miles S of Colchester at **Fingringhoe,** is part of the Essex Wildlife Trust. Easy to follow background information on the plants and animals to be seen along the nature trails. Wildlife Discovery Days for 8-11 year olds all school hols. Open daily, 9am-5pm. Closed Mons, 25th-26th Dec. Open Bank Hol Mons. 01206 729678. www.essexwt.org.uk

Map Ref: Grid square on Page 2 Map   Schools: Facilities available   ● Birthday parties

Free Places

B3 | Schools, Open all year (ERS) | **Hadleigh Castle Country Park,** Chapel Lane, **Hadleigh,** off A13, has plenty of countryside to enjoy with fine views over the Thames estuary and marshes. Nearby are the remains of an ancient castle. Open daily, 8am-dusk. 01702 551072. www.essexcc.gov.uk/countryparks

Schools, Open all year | **High Woods Country Park,** Colchester, enjoys a varied range of habitats: woodlands, grassland, lake, marsh and farmland. Excellent Visitors' Centre and a Ranger Service provides talks, guided walks and superb schools education service. Car park open 7am-10pm Summer, 7am-7pm Winter. Visitor Centre open daily, Apr-Sept, weekends only Oct-Mar. 01206 853588.

Schools, Open all year | **Ipswich Museum,** High Street, has a splendid collection of British natural history, world folklore and a vivid "Romans in Suffolk" exhibition. The Victorian Natural History Gallery has been recreated as it opened in 1881. Schools by appointment. Open Tues-Fri, 10am-5pm. Sat 10am-4.45pm. Closed Good Fri and Christmas. 01473 433550. www.ipswich.gov.uk

Open all year | **Lexden Park,** Colchester, is a designated nature reserve in old parkland with a lake, grassland and woodland. Open daily, 8.30am-dusk. 01206 282222.

Schools, Open all year | **Natural History Museum,** All Saints Church, **Colchester,** opposite the Castle, has "hands-on" displays of the fascinating natural history of NE Essex. Open Mon-Sat, 10am-5pm, Sun, 11am-5pm. Closed Christmas. 01206 282941. www.colchestermuseums.org.uk

Open all year | **Needham Lake,** Needham Market, is a beautiful lake with picnic benches, nature areas and play equipment. The lake is used for fishing, sailing and model boats. Permits are available from the Council Offices, Needham Market. 01449 720711.

Open all year | **Nowton Park,** Bury St Edmunds, has acres of glorious landscape, meadows and picnic areas, also way-marked walks.

Open all year | **Recreation Ground,** Vista Road, **Clacton-on-Sea,** has an adventure playground with a good range of equipment.

Schools | **Tymperleys Clock Museum,** Trinity Street, **Colchester,** displays a fine collection of locally made timepieces. Open Apr-Oct, Mon-Sat, 10am-5pm, Sun 11am-5pm. 01206 282943. www.colchestermuseums.org.uk

Open all year | **West Stow Country Park,** West Stow, off A1101. A 125 acre park and Site of Special Scientific Interest, offering a variety of Breckland Habitats, nature trail, hides, woodland, river and lake and excellent play area. Visitors' Centre, cafeteria and shop. (Access to Anglo-Saxon Village - see "Historic Sites" chapter). Open 10am-5pm Winter, 8pm Summer. 01284 728718. www.stedmundsbury.gov.uk/weststow

4 | Schools, Open all year | **Beecroft Art Gallery,** Station Road, **Westcliff.** Permanent display from 16th to 20th centuries and a changing programme of temporary exhibitions, including an annual schools exhibition. Open Tues-Sat, 9.30am-1pm, 2-5pm. Closed Bank Hol Mons and 25th-26th Dec. 01702 347418. www.beecroft-art-gallery.co.uk

Schools | **Bradwell Nuclear Power Station Visitor Centre,** Bradwell-on-Sea, Southminster, offers a friendly guided tour with multi media shows, interactive displays and even an animated model (site tours not for under 5s!). There is a picnic area and playground. Open Sun-Fri, Easter-Oct, 11am-5pm. It is best to prebook. 01621 873395. www.bnfl.com

Schools | **Castle Point Transport Museum,** 105 Point Road, **Canvey Island,** is run by volunteers who restore and look after a collection of commercial vehicles including fire engines, lorries, buses and coaches. Rides available at the Transport Show, 2nd Sun in Oct for which there is an entrance charge. Open Suns, Apr-Oct, 10am-5pm. (Other times by arrangement for pre-booked parties.) 01268 684272. www.topolino.demon.co.uk/

Map Ref: Grid square on Page 2 Map   Schools: Facilities available   ● Birthday parties

MAP REFS

B4 Schools, Open all year — **Central Museum,** Victoria Avenue, **Southend,** has a fantastic new Discovery Centre with a hands-on approach. Topic tables, handling trays and topic trays. Also features video microscopes and Southend Image Database (S.I.D.), holding 500 local images which can be printed off. Open Tues-Sat, 10am-5pm. Closed Bank Hols. 01702 434449. www.southendmuseums.co.uk

Schools, Open all year (ERS) — **Cudmore Grove Country Park,** East Mersea, approached from Broman's Lane, has grassland, popular for picnics. Access to the shore, with views over the Colne estuary. Hide for good birdwatching. Guided walks etc. Open daily, 8am-dusk. 01206 383868. www.essexcc.gov.uk/countryparks

Open all year — **Danbury Common,** NT, **Danbury,** near Chelmsford. Large area of common with coppice woodland and lowland heath, dating back to medieval times. Plenty of waymarked paths. Donations welcomed.

Schools, Open all year (ERS) — **Danbury Country Park,** Sandon Road, **Danbury,** is a small country park rich in wildlife. There are lakes with fishing, ornamental gardens and woodland. Open daily, 8am-dusk. 01245 222350. www.essexcc.gov.uk/countryparks

Schools, Open all year — **East Essex Aviation Society Museum,** Martello Tower, **Point Clear.** This small but fascinating museum, housed in the old Martello Tower, is packed full of artefacts and displays about both World Wars. There is a good view from the roof, but children under 14 must be accompanied by an adult. Open Mons, 7.30-9.30pm, Suns 10am-2pm, Bank Hols, 10am-4pm (also Weds, Jun-Sept 10am-2pm). Closed Christmas. Parties welcome at other times by arrangement. 01255 428028.

Open all year (ERS) — **Flitch Way Country Park,** following the disused railway line from **Braintree** to **Bishops Stortford** in Herts provides a trail for hikers, cyclists and horseriders. A Visitors' Centre housed in old railway station buildings at Rayne has a lively exhibition. Open daily, 9am-5pm. Exhibition and refreshments open Sun, 1-4pm, during Summer only. 01376 340262. www.essexcc.gov.uk/countryparks

Open all year — **Hockley Woods,** Hockley, has over 200 acres of woodlands with lovely walks, picnic area and a safely enclosed, well kept children's play area. Guided tours can be arranged. 01702 546466.

Open all year — **Hythe Quay,** Maldon. Stroll along the quay and see some fully restored traditional Thames Sailing Barges. 01621 856503.

Schools (ERS) — **Marsh Farm Country Park,** South **Woodham Ferrers,** is about 20 minutes walk from this new town. Motorists should follow the "Country Park and Open Farm" signs. The park includes an open-access commercial farm (entry charge) and a large nature reserve with riverside walks and picnic area. 01245 324191. (See also "Farms" chapter and Advert outside back cover.)

Schools, Open all year — **Northey Island,** NT, **Maldon,** is a wild and isolated island situated in the Blackwater estuary. Open to the public by appointment only, arrange with warden. Access on foot by a causeway which is cut off at high tide. 01621 853142.

Open all year — **Priory Park Playground,** Victoria Avenue, **Southend,** has a wide range of equipment including an embankment slide, rocking animals and swings.

Schools, Open all year — **Prittlewell Priory Museum,** Priory Park, Victoria Avenue, **Southend.** This 12th century monastery houses exhibits from local natural history to a collection of vintage radios. Both children and adults will enjoy having a go at the brass rubbing centre. Open Tues-Sat, 10am-5pm or dusk, closed 1-2pm. 01702 342878. www.southendmuseums.co.uk

Open all year — **Promenade Park,** Maldon. This attractive park by the Blackwater River has an adventure playground and marine lake for paddling and playing. Events are planned with the family in mind. 01621 856503.

Open all year — **Rayleigh Mount,** NT, **Rayleigh,** is a 4 acre site with a domesday motte and bailey castle erected by Sweyn of Essex. It is also managed for plants and wildlife. Open 7am-7.30pm (5pm in Winter).

Map Ref: Grid square on Page 2 Map   Schools: Facilities available   ● Birthday parties

Free Places

B4 Schools / Open all year — **Southchurch Hall**, Park Lane, **Southend**. Tucked away amid suburban houses, this moated, medieval manor house set in attractive gardens is well worth a visit. Excellent for schools. Open as Prittlewell Priory above. 01702 467671. www.southendmuseums.co.uk

Southchurch Park, Lifstan Way, **Southend-on-Sea**, has a children's playground, boating and model boat lakes.

Open all year — **Southend Pier**. Walk or ride the train. Various live entertainment for children throughout the Summer. Open daily, except 25th Dec. 01702 215622.

The Paddocks, **Canvey Island**, is an enclosed and supervised play area exclusively for under 8s. It includes play equipment, sandpit and climbing frames. Open Summer only.

Open all year — **Western Promenade Park**, **Brightlingsea**, has an open air paddling pool, boating lake and playground.

C1 Schools / Open all year — **Bacton Wood**, off B1150 near **North Walsham**, has waymarked trails and a permanent orienteering course. Education pack available. 01263 513811 ext. 6001.

Schools — **Toad Hole Cottage**, BA, How Hill, **Ludham**. This tiny eel-catcher's cottage, set in the fens, marshes and woodland of How Hill, recaptures the world of the Victorian marshman. Go on the walking and water trails - there is a small charge for a trip on the Electric Eel (see "Trips" chapter). (The house at How Hill is a broads Study Centre of interest to schools: 01692 678555.) Open daily, Apr-Oct; Apr-May, 11am-5pm; Jun-Sept, 10am-6pm; Oct, 11am-5pm. 01692 678763.

Open all year — **Winterton Dunes**. Large sand dune area with wide variety of coastal plants and birds.

C2 — **Berney Marshes**, RSPB, 4 miles W of **Great Yarmouth**. With no road access, this remote area of the Norfolk Broads, which often floods, can only be reached by boat or on foot by the Weavers Way. There are boat trips on the 1st Sun of each month from Burgh Castle at 10am and 2pm (pre-booking is required). 01493 700645.

Britannia Pier, Marine Parade, **Great Yarmouth**. A great place for a family day-out. With dodgems, ghost train, giant slide, bowling and amusement arcade, there is plenty to entertain the whole family. Complete the day with a show at the end-of-pier theatre. Rides are individually priced. Open Easter-Oct. Box Office, 01493 842209; General Office, 01493 842914.

Burgh Castle, EH, near **Great Yarmouth**. A short walk through windswept meadows brings you to the remains of one of a chain of Roman forts built to protect SE England. With its panoramic view, it's a perfect spot for a country picnic.

Schools — **Candlemaker & Model Centre**, **Stokesby**, off A1064 near Acle, boasts England's largest variety of handcrafted candles. Modelling kits available. Seasonal candle-dipping and fun activities during school holidays and weekends. (Small charge for activities.) Open Apr-Oct, Tues-Sun and Bank Hols, 9am-5.30pm; 1st Nov-mid Mar, Thurs-Sun, 10am-4pm; closed Christmas and Jan. 01493 750242.

Schools / Open all year — **Carlton Marshes Reserve**, **Carlton Colville**, near Lowestoft. A haven for wildlife in the Broads with an easy-to-follow nature trail and lots of interesting displays at the Visitors' Centre. Open daily. Visitors' Centre open Apr-Oct, Mon-Fri, 3-5pm, Sat & Sun 2-5pm; Sept-Mar, weekends only, but other times by arrangement. 01502 564250. www.wildlifetrust.org.uk/suffolk

Schools — **Laxfield and District Museum**, Guildhall, High St. A fascinating display of social history housed in the 16th century Guildhall. Includes a Victorian kitchen, costumes and farm implements. Open May-end Sept, weekends and Bank Hols, 2-5pm. Pre-booked parties by arrangement at other times. 01986 798460/798421.

Map Ref: Grid square on Page 2 Map   Schools: Facilities available   ● Birthday parties

| MAP REFS | PRICE CODES |

C2

"Little Tern Project", RSPB, North Denes, **Great Yarmouth**. From May-mid Aug, watch the little terns nesting on the beach. Around mid Jun, the chicks begin to hatch and entertain children and adults alike, by running around the beach. 01603 715191.

Schools **Lowestoft Museum,** Nicholas Everitt Park. Exhibits cover local and domestic history. Donations welcomed. Opening times vary. 01502 511457.

Open all year **Nicholas Everitt Park,** Oulton Broad, near Lowestoft, is a bustling watery place. Enjoy the boating and play centre with trampolines, crazy golf and playground. Power boat racing some Thurs evenings in Summer.

Schools **Norfolk and Suffolk Aviation Museum,** Flixton, on the B1026 near Bungay has a collection of aircraft on display, restored by an enthusiastic band of volunteers. Indoor display of items relating to history of aviation. Open Easter-mid Sept, Sun-Thurs, 10am-5pm; mid Winter, Sun-Wed, 10am-5pm. 01502 714726.

Schools **North West Tower,** BA, North Quay, **Great Yarmouth**. Built in 1344 as part of the town walls of Great Yarmouth, the Tower is now a Broads information centre, with historical exhibits, souvenirs and guide books. Climb the spiral stairs for fantastic views across Breydon Water, and operate a film projector loaded with archive film. Open daily, Jul-Sept. 10am-3.45pm. 01493 332095.

Schools **Seething Airfield Control Tower,** Station 146, Seething Airfield, **Seething**. Renovated original World War II control tower. On display are exhibits, photographs, war diaries and stories relating to the men of the 448th Bomb Group, who were stationed here during the war. Refreshments available. Open first Sun of month, May-Oct, 10am-5pm. 01508 550787. www.seething.org.uk

Open all year **Ted Ellis Trust,** Wheatfen Broad, **Surlingham**. 130 acres of marsh and woodland on the river Yare, with waymarked footpaths and hides. Wild, remote and muddy! Open dawn to dusk. 01508 538036.

C3

Schools *Open all year* **Dunwich Heath and Minsmere Beach,** NT, **Saxmundham**. A remnant of the once extensive Sandlings heaths. Many excellent walks and a good beach. There is an observation room, tearoom and shop (please call for opening times). Heath Barn Study Centre. Open daily dawn to dusk. 01728 648505/648501.

Schools *Open all year* **Dunwich Museum,** St. James Street. This small but fascinating museum shows how a once major port disappeared into the sea. Small charge for school parties. Open Mar weekends 2-4.30pm, Apr-end Sept, daily, 11.30am-4.30pm, Oct, 12-4pm, off season by appointment. 01728 648796.

Schools *Open all year* **Foxburrow Farm,** Saddlemakers La, **Melton**, is owned by the Suffolk Wildlife Trust and is a wildlife haven within a working arable farm, complete with farm trail. A whole host of activities is on offer for visiting school groups. Special events all year. Open daily. 01394 380113. www.wildlifetrust.org.uk/suffolk/videx.htm

Schools *Open all year* **Landguard Point,** Viewpoint Rd, **Felixstowe**. Situated on a shingle peninsula at the southern end of Felixstowe, this reserve is a haven for rare coastal plants and nationally important for migrating birds. Special events all year. Open daily. 01394 673782.

Schools *Open all year* **Valley Farm White Animal Collection,** Wickham Market, has Britain's only herd of breeding Camargue horses from the south of France. Other white animals include Muffin the Mule and Baa Baa the sheep. There are also pony and trap rides by prior arrangement. Donations welcome. Small charge for schools. Open daily 10am-4pm, closed Christmas and New Year. 01728 746916. www.valleyfarm.demon.co.uk

Map Ref: Grid square on Page 2 Map   Schools: Facilities available   ● Birthday parties

Directory of Activities and Information

General abbreviations used in addresses within the listings are as follows: Ave.: Avenue, Clo.: Close, Cresc.: Crescent, Dri.: Drive, Gdns.: Gardens, Gr.: Green, Gro.: Grove, La.: Lane, Pk.: Park, Pl.: Place, RG.: Recreation Ground, Rd.: Road, Sq.: Square, St.: Street, Tce.: Terrace.
Abbreviations specific to a particular section are listed at the beginning of that section.

ADVENTURE ACTIVITIES

B1 Brancaster Staithe, NT, **Brancaster Millennium Activity Centre**, Dial House. See "Farms" chapter. 01485 210719.

Sheringham, **Hilltop Outdoor Centre**, Old Wood, Beeston Regis. 01263 824514.

C2 Filby, **Norfolk Youth & Community Service**, Outdoor Education Programme. 01493 368129.

BICYCLE HIRE

A1 Great Bircham, **Great Bircham Windmill**. 01485 578393.

Heacham, **A. E. Wallis**, 34 High St. 01485 571683.

Hunstanton, **Fat Birds Don't Fly**, Cycle Centre, 22 Greevegate. 01485 535875.

A2 Cambridge, **Geoffs Bike Hire**, 65 Devonshire Rd., nr. railway station. 01223 365629.

A4 Highams Park, **Heales Cycles**, 477, Hale End Rd. 020 8527 1592.

B1 Aylsham, **Huff & Puff Cycle Hire**, at Bure Valley Railway. 01263 732935.

Cromer, **Knight Riders**, Gordon House, West St. 01263 510039.

Reepham, **Reepham Station**, Station Rd. 01603 871187.

Sheringham, **Bike Riders**, 7 St Peters Rd. 01263 821906.

B2 Thetford Forest Park, **High Lodge Forest Centre**. 01842 810090.

B3 Stutton, **Alton Cycle Hire**, Holbrook Rd, Alton Reservoir. 01473 283773.

C1 Hoveton, **Broadland Cycle Hire**, The Rhond. 01603 783096.

Ludham, **Ludham Bridge Boat Services**. 01692 630486/630322.

North Walsham, **Bike Riders**, 3 Market St. 01692 406632.

MAP REFS

C1 Sutton, **Sutton Staithe Boatyard**. 01692 581653.

C2 Loddon, **Broadland Riverine Boatcraft**, Loddon Boatyard. 01508 528735. www.riverine.co.uk

Stokesby, **Riverside Tearoom and Stores**. 01493 750470.

C3 Darsham, **Byways Bikes**, nr. Yoxford, off A12. Closed Tues. 01728 668764.

BOAT HIRE

Abbreviations: C: Canoes, DC: Day Cruisers, M: Motor boats, P: Pedalos, R: Rowing boats, SE: Self drive electric boats.

A3 Cambridge, **River Cam**. C, R. Try your hand at punting, available at various points on the river. 01223 301845. (See also "Trips" chapter for chauffeur punts.)

A4 Broxbourne, **Lee Valley Boat Centre**. M, R. 01992 462085.

Ilford, **Fairlop Waters**. C, R. 020 8501 1833.

Thurrock, **Lakeside Diving and Watersports Centre**. P, R. 01708 860947.

B2 Brandon, **Bridge House**. M, R. 01842 813137.

Norwich, **Griffin Lane**, Thorpe St. Andrew. C, M. 01603 701701.

B3 Aldham, **Mill Race Nurseries**. R. 01206 242521.

C1 Coltishall, Wroxham Rd. C, P, R, SE. 07887 504947.

Hickling, Staithe Rd. M, R, S. 01692 598314.

Horning, **Ferry Boatyard**. DC, M. 01692 630392.

Ludham Bridge. M. 01692 630486. www.ludhambridgeboats.co.uk

Wroxham, Riverside Rd. M 01603 782625/782333. Riverside Rd DC. 01603 782527. Staitheway Rd. DC. 01603 783311. The Bridge. M, SE. 01603 782207. www.broads.co.uk The Bridge. M. 01603 783043.

C2 Acle, Acle Bridge. DC. 01493 750378.

Brundall, Riverside Estate. M. 01603 715048. Riverside Estate. DC. 01603 715011. Riverside Estate. DC. 01603 713546.

Bungay, **Outney Meadow Caravan Park**. C, R. 01986 892338.

Map Ref: Grid square on page 2 map. ✦ Birthday parties organised.

C2 Geldeston, **Wherry Dyke**. C. 01508 518208.
Great Yarmouth, **North Drive Boating Lake**. C, P, R.
Loddon. C, DC, R. 01508 528735. www.riverine.co.uk
Lowestoft, **Nicholas Everitt Park**, Oulton Broad. R.
Potter Heigham, **The Bridge**. M, SE. 01692 670711. www.broads.co.uk **Riverside**. M. 01692 670241.
Smallburgh. C, DC. 01692 582457.
St Olaves, Reeds Lane. 01493 488675.
Stalham, **The Staithe**. DC, M. 01692 580288. **The Staithe**. DC. 01692 581081.
Sutton Staithe. C. 01692 581653.
Wayford Bridge, **Staithe Cottage**. C, DC. 01692 582071/582457.

C3 Thorpeness, **Thorpeness Mere**. C, R. 01728 832523.

BOWLING (TEN PIN)

A1 Hunstanton, **Thomas's Entertainment**, The Showboat, Le Strange Tce. 01485 532377.
♦ King's Lynn, **Strikes Bowl Multiplex**, 1-5 Lynn Rd, Gaywood. 01553 760333.

A3 Bishop's Stortford, **Bowl Xtra**, Anchor St. 01279 755204.

A4 ♦ Basildon, **Hollywood Bowl**, Festival Leisure Park. 01268 531122.
♦ Chelmsford, **Megabowl**, Widford Industrial Estate. 01245 359249.
♦ Dagenham, **Superbowl**, New Rd. 020 8592 0347.
♦ Harlow, **Firstbowl**, 33B Terminus St. 01279 418841.
♦ Romford, **City Limits**, Collier Row Rd. 020 8598 9888 / 020 8924 4000.

B1 Fakenham, **Superbowl**, Bridge St. 01328 856650.
Wells-next-the-Sea, **Playland** Quayside. 01328 711656/710461.

B2 ♦ Norwich, **Hollywood Bowl**, Riverside Leisure Park, Wherry Rd. 01603 631311. **Number Ten**, 10 Barnard Rd, Bowthorpe. 01603 740730.

B3 ♦ Bury St. Edmunds, **Bury Bowl**, Eastgate St. 01284 750704.
♦ Colchester, **Megabowl**, off Cowdray Ave. 01206 560500.
♦ Ipswich, **Kingpin Bowl**, Martlesham Heath.
♦ 01473 611111. **Solar Bowl**, Sproughton Rd. 01473 241242.

B3 ♦ Sudbury, **Sudbury Bowl**, Byford Rd. 01787 312288.

B4 ♦ Southend-on-Sea, **The Kursaal**, Eastern Esplanade. 01702 322322.

C1 ♦ North Walsham, **Strikers**, Tungate Farm, Tungate. 01692 407793.

C2 ♦ Great Yarmouth, **Regent Bowl**, 92 Regent Rd. 01493 856830.

C3 ♦ Walton-on-the-Naze, **Walton Pier Ten Pin Bowling Centre**. 01255 675646.

BRASS RUBBING

B1 Blickling Church. See under **Blickling Park** in "Free Places" chapter.

C2 Great Yarmouth, **Tolhouse Museum**, Tolhouse St. 01493 745526.

BUYING FURNITURE

Tewin, **'Tots to Teens Furniture'**, The Old Dairy, Tewin Hill Farm, Tewin Hill, Nr Welwyn Garden City. Just over the border in Herts, this South East specialist offers an outstanding selection from nursery through to adult, of beds and furniture from own range and brand names "Heather Spencer", "Flexa", "Thuka", "Paidi" and more. Just 5 mins from Jn 6, A1 which is just 20 mins from Jn 23 M25. Please phone for location map. 07957 870043. (See Advert page 28.)

CINEMAS

A1 King's Lynn, **Majestic**, Tower St. 01553 772603.

A3 Bishop's Stortford, **Ciniworld**, Anchor St 01279 659301/Booking: 710000.
Cambridge, **Arts Picture House**, 38/39 St Andrews St. 01223 504444.

A4 Basildon, **UCI.**, Festival Leisure Park 08700 102030.
Chelmsford, **Odeon**, The Meadows. 01245 348494/08705 050007.
Edmonton, **UCI.**, Picketts Lock Leisure Centre. 08700 102030.
♦ Harlow, **U.G.C.**, Queensgate Centre. 01279 436014/0870 9070713. **Odeon**, The High 08705 050007/01279 433550.
Romford, **Ster Century**, 1-15 The Brewery 01708 759100.
Thurrock Lakeside, **Warner Cinema**. 01708 890568. **UCI.** 08700 102030.

B1 Cromer, **Regal**, Hans Pl. 01263 513311.

B2 Dereham, **Hollywood Cinema**, Market Place 01362 691133.

Map Ref: Grid square on page 2 map. ♦ Birthday parties organised.

Directory of Activities & Information

MAP REFS

B2 Norwich, Cinema City, St. Andrew's St. 01603 622047. Hollywood Cinema, Anglia Sq. 01603 621903. Ster Century, Castle Mall. 01603 221900. UCI, Riverside, 08700 102030.

B3 Bury St. Edmunds, ABC, Hatter St. 01284 754477/762586/705400.
Colchester, Odeon, Crouch St. 08705 050 007/01206 544869.
Halstead, Empire, Beridge Rd. 01787 477001/478308.
Harwich, Electric Palace, Kings Quay. 01255 553333.
Ipswich, Film Theatre, Corn Exchange. 01473 433100/433133. Odeon, St. Margaret's St. 01473 287287/08705 050007.
Stowmarket, Regal Theatre, Ipswich St. 01449 612825. U.G.C., Cardinal Park. 0870 907 0748/01473 254978.

B4 Burnham-on-Crouch, Rio, High St. 01621 782027.
Canvey Island, Movie Starr, Eastern Esplanade. 01268 695000.
Clacton-on-Sea, Flix, 129 Pier Ave. 01255 421188/429627.
Southend-on-Sea, Odeon, Victoria Circus. 01702 393543/08705 050007.
South Woodham Ferrers, Flix, Market Sq. 01245 329777/325511.

C2 Great Yarmouth, Hollywood Cinema, Marine Pde. 01493 842043.
Lowestoft, Marina, The Marina. 01502 573318. Hollywood, London Rd. South. 01502 588355/564567.

C3 Aldeburgh, Aldeburgh Cinema, 51 High St. 01728 452996.
Felixstowe, The Palace, Crescent Rd. 01394 274455/671330.
Leiston, Film Theatre, High St. 01728 830549.
Woodbridge, Riverside, Quayside. 01394 382174.

CRAZY GOLF

A1 Hunstanton, Esplanade Gdns.

A4 Brentwood, King George's Playing Field. 01277 214830.

B3 Colchester, Castle Park.

B4 Clacton, Marine Parade East.

C2 Fritton, Caldecott Hall Country Club. 01493 488535.
Great Yarmouth, Marine Pde. Pirates Cove, (between Marina Centre & Britannia Pier). Nelson Gdns, (between Wellington Pier & Pleasure Beach).
Lowestoft, Nicholas Everitt Park.

MAP REFS

C3 Felixstowe, Mannings Amusement Park. 01394 282370.

HELPING GREAT ORMOND STREET

2002 is the 150th Anniversary!

Great Ormond Street Hospital Children's Charity needs everyone's support to help raise £12 million each year. There are many ways to get involved raising money to help buy medical equipment, fund pioneering research and provide support services for the young patients and their families. Look out for the many special 150th Birthday events throughout the year, see below. Unless otherwise stated, call GOSH fundraising on

0207 916 5678 or log onto www.gosh.org You can make a difference.

GOSH Concert on 10th April is a special classical concert at The Barbican Theatre featuring Chloe. Box office 020 7638 8891 for tickets and information.

GOSH Abseil on 8th June where over 10's can join the world record holding team as they attempt another record. Also look out for Junior Abseil in Sept. Ask for Matt Forrest.

Summer in the City planned for 6th July. A great football-themed day out for all the family. Ask for Karen Phillips.

Kid's Nosh for GOSH throughout 2002. Organise your own tea party for friends and family and help raise money. Information packs from Cherie Murphy.

Jeans for Genes Day is 4th Oct. Wear your jeans to school for a £1 donation and help raise money for children with genetic disorders. Call 0800 980 4800 for an activity pack.

Get your school involved throughout the year with the GOSH "Mathathon", "Spellathon" or "Make-A-Face" challenge. Ask for Sylvia Iyeke.

ICE SKATING

A4 ✦ Leyton, Lee Valley Ice Centre, Lea Bridge Rd. 020 8533 3155.
✦ Romford, Ice Arena, Rom Valley Way. 01708 724731.
✦ Chelmsford, Riverside Ice and Leisure Centre, Victoria Rd. 01245 615050.

Map Ref: Grid square on page 2 map.   ✦ Birthday parties organised.

MAP REFS

KARTING

A3 Haverhill, Rookwood Way. 01440 763738.

A4 ✦ Brentwood, Brentwood Park Karting. 01277 260001.

B1 Cromer, Karttrak, The Avenue, Northrepps. 01603 486655.

✦ Sheringham, Cub Karting, 20 Nelson Rd. 01263 821950.

B2 Norwich, Indoor Kart Centre, Vulcan Rd North. 01603 486655.

Swaffham, Anglia Karting Centre, The Airfield, N. Pickenham. 01760 441777.

✦ Wymondham, Kids Karts and The Karting Company, Elm Farm, Norwich Common. 01953 604705.

B3 ✦ Colchester, Indikart, Whitehall Industrial Estate, Grange Way. 01206 799511.

Ipswich, Anglia Indoor Kart Racing, Farthing Rd. 01473 240087.

B4 Rayleigh, Rayleigh Indoor Karting, Brook Rd. 01268 777765.

C2 ✦ Great Yarmouth, Karting 2000, Trafalgar Wks, Fermer Rd. 01493 854041.

LASER FUN

A3 ✦ Cambridge, Laserquest, 2nd Floor, 13-15 Bradwells Court. 01223 302102.

A4 ✦ Chelmsford, Megazone, New Writtle St. 01245 347333.

B2 ✦ Norwich, Megazone Laser Adventure, 17-19 St Stephens Rd. 01603 763403.

B3 Colchester, Quasar at Rollerworld, Eastgates. 01206 868868.

✦ Ipswich, Megazone at Jim's Totally Brilliant Ltd., Whitehouse Rd. 01473 464616.

Stowmarket, Laser Maze at Mid Suffolk Leisure Centre, Gainsborough Rd. 01449 742817.

B4 ✦ Rayleigh, Megazone, 7 Brook Rd. 01268 779100.

Southend-on-Sea, Mr B's Quasar Spacechase, 5-9 Marine Pde. 01702 603947.

C2 Great Yarmouth, Quasar at The Mint, 31 Marine Pde. 01493 332656.

LOCAL COUNCILS

ESSEX LOCAL AUTHORITIES
Essex County Council 01245 492211
www.essexcc.gov.uk
Basildon, 01268 533333
Braintree, 01376 552525
Brentwood, 01277 261111

MAP REFS

Castle Point, 01268 882200
Chelmsford, 01245 606606
Colchester, 01206 282222
Epping Forest, 01992 564000
Harlow, 01279 446611
Maldon, 01621 854477
Rochford, 01702 546366
Southend-on-Sea, 01702 215000
Tendring, 01255 425501
Thurrock, 01375 390000
Uttlesford, 01799 510510

NORFOLK LOCAL AUTHORITIES
Norfolk County Council 01603 222222
www.norfolk.gov.uk
Breckland, 01842 755721
Broadland, 01603 431133
Great Yarmouth, 01493 856100
King's Lynn & West Norfolk, 01553 692722
North Norfolk, 01263 513811
Norwich City Council, 01603 622233
South Norfolk, 01508 533633

SOUTH CAMBS LOCAL AUTHORITIES
Cambridgeshire County Council 01223 717111 www.cambridgeshire.gov.uk
Cambridge City Council, 01223 457000
South Cambridgeshire District Council, 01223 443000

SUFFOLK LOCAL AUTHORITIES
Suffolk County Council 01473 583000
www.suffolkcc.gov.uk
Babergh, 01473 822801
Forest Heath, 01638 719000
Ipswich, 01473 432000
Mid Suffolk, 01449 720711
St. Edmundsbury, 01284 763233
Suffolk Coastal, 01394 383789
Waveney, 01502 562111

MAIZE MAZE

A3 Widdington, Mole Hall Wildlife Park, Easter-end Oct. 01799 540400. (See Advert page 65.)

B1 South Creake, Compton Hall. Mid-Jul to mid-Sept. 01328 823224.

MUSIC & MOVEMENT

Jo Jingles classes are run in many areas 01494 676575. (See Advert and information in centre section

---

Map Ref: Grid square on page 2 map.   ✦ Birthday parties organised.

PITCH AND PUTT

A1 Hunstanton, Cromer Rd.

B2 Norwich, Eaton Park, South Park Ave. 01603 454401. Mousehold Heath, Gurney Rd. 01603 419200.
Wymondham, Silfield Village Pitch & Putt course. 01953 603508.

B3 Ipswich, Chantry Park.
Sudbury, Belle Vue Park. 07765 421899.

B4 Clacton, Happy Valley, Holland Rd.
Southend, Belfairs Park. 01702 525345.

C2 Great Yarmouth, Bure Park, Caister Rd. 01493 843621.
Lowestoft, Dip Farm, Corton Rd. 01502 513322.

PLAY CENTRES

Abbreviations: LC: Leisure Centre, SC: Sports Centre

A1 King's Lynn, Strikes Bowl Multiplex, 1-5 Lynn Rd, Gaywood. 01553 760333.

A2 ✦ Mildenhall, Pirate Island at The Dome LC, Bury Rd. 01638 717737.

A3 ✦ Braintree, Smugglers Cove at The Riverside Centre, St. John Ave. 01376 323240.
✦ Cambridge, Magic Kingdom at Abbey Pool, Whitehall Rd. 01223 213352.
✦ Haverhill, KidZown at Haverhill LC, Ehringshausen Way. 01440 702548.

A4 ✦ Chelmsford, Kool Kids at Riverside Ice & LC, Victoria Rd. 01245 615050.
Thurrock, Belmont Village Hall, Kenningtons Centre, Orchard Centre, Purfleet Centre, Tilbury Centre, West Thurrock Centre. 01375 652300.

B1 ✦ Cromer, Funstop, Exchange House, Louden Rd. 01263 514976. (See "Theme Parks" chapter.)
✦ Fakenham, Megafun at Superbowl, Bridge St. 01328 856650.

B2 ✦ Attleborough, KoolKidz, 34/35 Haverscroft Industrial Estate. 01953 457333.
✦ Norwich, Bedlam, Unit H1, Fifer's Lane Trading Estate, Union Park. 01603 427756; 70 Castle Mall. 01603 622561. Jumping Jacks at Norwich Sport Village, Drayton High Rd, Hellesdon. 01603 788898/788912.
✦ Wymondham, Funtime Factory, Ayton Rd. 01953 608080.

B3 Ipswich, Landseer Play Centre, Hogarth Rd., is a purpose-built play centre offering free activities all year to 6-14 year olds. 01473 433661. (See Advert page 22.)
✦ Stowmarket, Ocean Adventure at Mid Suffolk LC, Gainsborough Rd. 01449 742817.

B4 ✦ Witham, Pirates Paradise at Bramston SC, Bridge St. 01376 519200.

C1 ✦ Knapton, Elephant Playbarn, Mundesley Rd. 01263 721080. (See "Theme Parks" chapter.)

C3 ✦ Felixstowe, Funtasia at Felixstowe LC, Undercliff Rd West. 01394 670411.

POTTERY PAINTING

A3 Bishop's Stortford, The Glaze Box, 7 South Street, Commercial Centre. 01279 467396.
Cambridge, Glaze to Amaze, 54 Burleigh St. 01223 319600.

B3 Bury St Edmunds, Glaze to Amaze, 100 Risbygate St. 01284 756666.

PUTTING GREENS

A1 Hunstanton, Esplanade Gdns.

A4 Billericay, Lake Meadows Recreation Ground.

B2 Norwich, Mousehold Heath, Eaton Park and Waterloo Park, Angel Road. 01603 212145.

B3 Bury St. Edmunds, Abbey Gardens. 01284 757490.
Colchester, Castle Park.
Ipswich, Chantry Park.
Sudbury, Belle Vue Park. 07765 421899.

C2 Fritton, Caldecott Hall Country Club. 01493 488535.
Gorleston, Marine Parade.

C2 Lowestoft, Denes Oval. Kirkley Cliff, on seafront.
Oulton Broad, Nicholas Everitt Park.

ROLLER SKATING, BOARDING & BMX

Abbreviations: RB: Roller blading, RS: Roller skating, SB: Skate boarding

A2 ✦ Wisbech, Skaters, Mill Rd, Walpole Highway. RS. 01945 880324.

A4 Stratford, Lee Valley Cycle Centre. Quarter Mile La. Booking advisable. BMX. 020 8534 6085.

Map Ref: Grid square on page 2 map. ✦ Birthday parties organised.

B2 ✦ **Norwich, SolarSkate,** Spar Rd, off Vulcan Rd. RS. 01603 403220. **Norwich Skate Park,** Queens Rd. BMX, RB, SB. 01603 611699.
Sloughbottom Park. Cycle Speedway. 01603 212145.

B3 ✦ **Colchester, Rollerworld,** Eastgates. RS. 01206 868868.
Dovercourt, Lower Marine Parade, RS. In Summer only.

SNOW SPORTS

A4 ✦ **Brentwood, Brentwood Park Dry Ski Centre,** Warley Gap. 01277 211994.

B2 ✦ **Norwich, Norfolk Ski Club,** Whitlingham La, Trowse. 01603 662781.

B3 ✦ **Ipswich, Suffolk Ski Centre,** Bourne Hill, Wherstead. 01473 602347.

SPECTATOR SPORTS

A1 **King's Lynn, Saddlebow Speedway.** Speedway, go-cart and stock car racing. 01553 771111.

A4 **Purfleet, Arena Essex.** Speedway, banger, stock car and hot rod racing. 01708 867728.

B2 **Horsford, Norfolk County Cricket Club,** Manor Park Sports Ground, Holt Rd. 01603 748810.

✦ **Norwich City Football Club,** Carrow Rd. 01603 760760. Football in the Community activities and birthday parties, 01603 761122.

Snetterton Racing Circuit, Snetterton. British Touring Cars and British Superbike. 01953 887303. Tickets, 0870 6060611.

Swaffham Stadium. Spedeworth International. See editorial under Ipswich B3 and Advert page 25.

B3 ✦ **Colchester, Colchester United Football Club,** Layer Rd. 01206 508800/508802. Birthday parties 01206 572378.

✦ **Ipswich, Ipswich Town Football Club,** Portman Rd. 01473 400500.

Spedeworth International at Foxhall Heath Raceway, Foxhall Stadium, **Ipswich**, presents a motor extravaganza with a range of action packed meetings to excite and entertain the whole family. The action on the track varies from event to event, with well known drivers from the UK and around the world. As brightly coloured bangers roar around the oval raceway, crashes and smashes are all part of the experience, but the safety of participants and spectators is

paramount. Some meeting have pre-event entertainment, celebrities, prizes and a fireworks finale. Race days are on Saturday evenings and some Sundays. Spedeweekends in July. Please call for confirmation on 09003 421 621. www.stockcar.co.uk (See Advert page 25.)

SPORTS & LEISURE CENTRES

Abbreviations: LC: Leisure Centre, LCb: Leisure Club, LCx: Leisure Complex, LP: Leisure Park, RC: Recreation Centre, SC: Sports Centre, SCC: Sports & Conference Centre, SH: Sports Hall.
*Centre has a swimming pool.

A1 ✦ **Hunstanton, Oasis LC*,** Central Promenade. 01485 534227.

✦ **King's Lynn, Lynnsport & LP,** Greenpark Ave. 01553 818001.

✦ **King's Lynn SC,** Gaywood Rd. 01553 760923.

A2 ✦ **Mildenhall, Dome LC,** Bury Rd. 01638 717737.

A3 ✦ **Bottisham, SC*,** Lode Rd. 01223 811121/812148.

✦ **Braintree, Braintree LC,** Panfield La. 01376 552585. **Notley SC,** Notley Rd. 01376 323873. **Riverside Centre*,** St. John Ave 01376 323240. **Towerlands,** Panfield Rd 01376 326802.

✦ **Cambridge, Kelsey Kerridge SC,** Queen Anne Tce. 01223 462226.

✦ **Great Dunmow, SC*,** Parsonage Downs 01371 873782.

✦ **Haverhill, LC*,** Ehringshausen Way. 01440 702548.

✦ **Newmarket, LC,** Exning Rd. 01638 662726 **Saffron Walden, Lord Butler LC*,** Peaslands Rd. 01799 522777.

A3 **South Cambridgeshire.** The Village College facilities are dual use and vary from site to site. They are usually open to the public the evenings and at weekends. Ring daytime to check.

Bassingbourn Village College 01763 24613 **Bottisham Village College*** 01223 81112 **Comberton Village College** 01223 26250 **Cottenham Village College** 01954 28894 **Gamlingay Village College** 01767 65178 **Impington Village College** 01223 20040 **Linton Village College** 01223 89024 **Melbourne Village College*** 0176 260566/263313. **Sawston Village College** 01223 712555. **Swavesey Village College** 01954 230366.

Map Ref: Grid square on page 2 map. ✦ Birthday parties organised.

Directory of Activities & Information

MAP REFS

A4
- Basildon, Basildon SC, Nethermayne. 01268 533166. Markhams Chase SC, 01268 410126.
- Billericay, SC*, School Rd. 01277 655545.
- Brentwood, The Brentwood Centre*, Doddinghurst Rd., is a multi-purpose leisure complex with comprehensive outdoor facilities. It has both a main and learner pool, and runs coaching courses and "Splashtime" sessions throughout the year. The Centre is home to a variety of junior clubs with coaching available for badminton, gymnastics, tennis, football and trampoline. There is a brand new creche for 2-5 year olds and a fully supervised school holiday programme that caters for all ages, with a wonderful variety of activities. "Funtots" multi-activity sessions are available for pre-school children, "Jamboree" and "Games Galore" sessions for older children. Special events throughout the year include Roller Discos, Fancy Dress and Art Attacks. The recently launched club Y2K, promotes a healthier lifestyle for 12-16 year olds, where they can watch music and sports channels, or listen to music of their choice. For more information call 01277 215151. (See Advert page 20.)
- Brentwood, The Courage Hall, Middleton Hall La. 01277 227522.
- Chelmsford, Dovedale SC, Vicarage Rd. 01245 269020. Riverside Ice and LC*, Victoria Rd. 01245 615050.
- Chipping Ongar, LC*, Fyfield Rd. 01277 363969.
- Corringham, LC*, Springhouse Rd. 01375 678070.
- Epping, SC, 25 Hemnall St. 01992 564564. Grays, Blackshots LC*, Blackshots La. 01375 375533.

A4
- Harlow, Harlow SC, Hammarskjold Rd. 01279 307300. Latton Bush LC, Southern Way. 01279 446080. Norman Boot LC, Old Harlow, 01279 438199. Sumners LC, Broadley Rd. 01279 446266.
- Leyton, Lee Valley SC, 020 8519 0017.
- Loughton, Loughton Sports Centre (DCA) SH, Rectory La. 020 8508 4662.
- Pitsea, Eversley LC, 01268 583076.
- Shenfield, SC, Oliver Rd. 01277 226220. South Ockenden, Belhus Park LC*. 01708 856297/852248.
- Tilbury, LC, Brennan Rd. 01375 856886.
- Waltham Abbey, SC, Broomstick Hall Rd. 01992 716194.

MAP REFS

B1
- Fakenham, SC, Hempton Rd. 01328 862867. Sheringham, Pinewood Park LCb*, Holt Rd. 01263 821208. Splash LC*, Weybourne Rd. 01263 825675.

B2
- Brandon, LC, Church Rd, Remembrance Playing Field, 01842 813748.
- Bury St. Edmunds, LC*, Beetons Way. 01284 753496.
- Diss, Swim & Fitness LC*, Victoria Rd. 01379 652754.
- Easton SCC, Easton College. 01603 731208. Eye, SH, Hartismere High School, Castleton Way. 01379 870315.
- Long Stratton LC, Swan Lane. 01508 531444.
- Norwich, Blyth-Jex SC, Constitution Hill. 01603 427181. Bob Carter LC, School Rd, Drayton. 01603 867102. Norwich Sport Village and Aquapark*, Drayton High Rd., Hellesdon. 01603 788912. UEA Sports Park*, Earlham Rd. 01603 592398.
- Swaffham LC, Brandon Rd. 01760 723974.
- Thetford, Breckland LC & Waterworld*, Croxton Rd. 01842 753110.
- Wymondham LC*, Norwich Rd. 01953 607171.

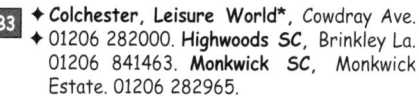

B3
- Colchester, Leisure World*, Cowdray Ave. 01206 282000. Highwoods SC, Brinkley La. 01206 841463. Monkwick SC, Monkwick Estate. 01206 282965.
- Debenham, LC, Gracechurch St. 01728 861101.
- Harwich, SC, Hall La., Dovercourt. 01255 504380.
- Halstead, SC, Colne Rd. 01787 472480.
- Ipswich. There are four sports centres run by Ipswich Borough Council. Each has an active programme for juniors and a wide choice of fun activities for every school holiday.
- Gainsborough SC, 5 Braziers Wood Rd, offers junior soccer, trampolining, badminton, gymnastics and a Rainbow Club for pre-schoolers. 01473 433644.
- Maidenhall SC, Maidenhall Approach, provides all the usual sports plus trampolining, junior soccer skills and tennis. During the school holidays a Day Camp is run where children can be left from 8.30am-5.15pm each day. 01473 433622.
- Northgate SC, Sidegate La. West, offers courses in 38 different activities including gymnastics and squash for all age groups. A Saturday morning club provides coaching in a range of sports. 01473 433611.

Map Ref: Grid square on page 2 map.   ♦ Birthday parties organised.

SOMETHING FOR THE KIDS

Activities for every holiday

MEGA WEEKS
MINI SPORTS COURSES
ART ATTACK
GAMES GALORE

JAMBOREE PLUS
TREASURE HUNT
ROLLER DISCO
JAMBOREE
AND LOTS MORE......

FOR MORE DETAILS PHONE (01277) 215151

BRENTWOOD CENTRE

Doddinghurst Road
Brentwood · Essex

www.brentwood-centre.co.uk

Directory of Activities & Information

MAP REFS	
B3	**Whitton SC**, Whitton Church La. has an extensive programme including soccer, gym, trampoline and cycle speedway. 01473 433633. The Council also operates an extensive sports development programme offering top quality coaching for youngsters throughout the year. Contact the Sport Development Office. 01473 433542. Enquiry @ipswich.gov.uk (See Advert page 22.)

+ **Manningtree, SC**, Colchester Rd, Lawford. 01206 393003.
+ **Stowmarket, Mid Suffolk LC***, Gainsborough Rd. 01449 674980.
  Sudbury, Great Cornard SC*, Head La.,
+ 01787 374861. **Sudbury SC**, Tudor Rd. 01787 373132.
  Tiptree, SC, Maypole Rd. 01621 817499.

B4
+ **Burnham-on-Crouch, Dengie Hundred SC**, Millfields. 01621 784633.
+ **Canvey Island, Waterside Farm SC***, Somnes Ave. 01268 694342.
+ **Clacton, LC***, Vista Rd. 01255 429647.
+ **Great Wakering, SC**, High St. 01702 219832.
+ **Hawkwell, Clements Hall LC***, Clements Hall Way. 01702 207777.
+ **Maldon, Blackwater LC***, Park Dr. 01621 851898.
+ **Rayleigh, Park SC**, Rawreth La. 01268 781233. **The Warehouse Centre RC**, 7 Brook Rd. 01268 779999/779100.

B4
  Shoeburyness, LC*, Delaware Rd. 01702 293558.
+ **Southend, Leisure and Tennis Centre**, Easter Ave. 01702 613000.
+ **South Woodham Ferrers, William de Ferrers SC**, Trinity Sq. 01245 329535.
+ **Westcliff-on-Sea, The Chase Sports & Fitness Centre**, Prittlewell Chase. 01702 433006.
+ **Wickford, Bromford SC**, Grange Ave. 01268 769369.
+ **Witham, Bramston SC***, Bridge St. 01376 519200.

C1
+ **Horning, Helska LC***, Horning Ferry, Marina Ferry Rd. 01692 630844.
  North Walsham SC, High School, Spenser Ave. 01692 402293.

C2
+ **Beccles, SC**, Ringsfield Rd. 01502 712039.
  Bungay, SH, Queen's Rd. 01986 894515.

MAP REFS	
C2	+ **Great Yarmouth, Marina LC***, Marine Pde. 01493 851521.

+ **Harleston Memorial LC**, Wilderness La. 01379 852088.
+ **Lowestoft, Waveney SC***, Water La. 01502 569116.
+ **Stalham, SH**, High School, Brumstead Rd. 01692 580864.
  Stradbroke, SH, Stradbroke High School. 01379 384387.

C3
+ **Felixstowe, LC***, Undercliff Rd. West. 01394 670411.
+ **Framlingham, SC**, Thomas Mills High School, Saxtead Rd. 01728 724374.
+ **Leiston, LC***, Redhouse La. 01728 830364.
  Woodbridge, Farlingaye SC, 01394 380323.

SWIMMING POOLS (INDOOR)

Please also check the list of Sports & Leisure Centres above. Those marked with an * have a pool.

A1 **King's Lynn, St James Indoor Swimming Pool**, Blackfriar's St. 01553 764888.

A2 **Downham Market Swimming Pool**, Lynn Road. 01366 383822.

+ **Mildenhall, Pool**, Recreation Way. 01638 712515.

A3
+ **Cambridge, Abbey Pool**, Whitehill Rd. 01223 213352.
+ **Newmarket, Pool**, High St. 01638 661736.

A4
+ **Basildon, Gloucester Park Pool**, Broadmayne. 01268 523588.
+ **Benfleet, Runnymede Pool**, Kiln Rd, Thundersley. 01268 756514.

A4 **Billericay, Pool**, Lake Meadows Pk. 01277 657111.

  Harlow, Stewards Pool, Pinceybrook Rd.,
+ **Staple Tye**. 01279 444503. **Harlow Pool**, First/Mandela Ave. 01279 446430.
+ **Leigh-on-Sea, Belfairs Swim Centre**, Fairview Gdns, off Eton Rd. 01702 712155.
+ **Pitsea, Pool**, Wickford Ave. 01268 556734. **Southend-on-Sea, Warrior Swim Centre**, Warrior Sq. 01702 464445.
+ **Waltham Abbey, Roundhills**. 01992 716733.

B1 **Aylsham Pool**, Sir Williams La. (Weekends only.) 01263 735040.

B2 **Barford Pool**, 48 Chapel St. 01603 758253. **Dereham Pool & Fitness Centre**, Quebec Rd. 01362 693419.
  Sprowston Swimming Pool and Sports Hall. (Weekends only.) 01603 487895.

Map Ref: Grid square on page 2 map.   + Birthday parties organised.

IPSWICH...
we're great sports...

find out more on
01473 433622

or visit our website
www.ibcsport.co.uk

MAP REFS

- **B2** ✦ Stradbroke Pool, Wilby Rd. 01379 384376.
- **B3** ✦ Hadleigh Leisure Pool, Stonehouse Rd. 01473 823470.
- ✦ Halstead Pool, Parsonage St. 01787 473706.
- ✦ Ipswich, Fore St Pool, Fore St. 01473 433668.
- **B4** ✦ Wickford Pool, Market Ave. 01268 765460.
- **C1** Bradwell, Phoenix Pool, off Mallard Way. 01493 664575.
- Hoveton, Broadland High School, Tunstead Rd. 01603 782715.
- **C2** Bungay, Waveney Valley Pool, St. John's Hill. 01986 895014.
- **C3** Dovercourt Pool, Wick La. 01255 508266.
- Woodbridge, Deben Swimming Pool, Station Rd. 01394 384763.

SWIMMING POOLS (OUTDOOR)

- **A1** Hunstanton, Oasis LC, Central Promenade. (Summer only.) 01485 534227.
- **A3** Cambridge, on Jesus Green. 01223 302579/213352.
- **A4** Chelmsford, Riverside Centre, Victoria Rd. 01245 615050.
- **B3** Ipswich, Broomhill Open Air Lido, Sherrington Rd. 01473 433655.
- Sudbury, Great Cornard SC, Head La. 01787 374861.
- **B4** Brightlingsea Pool, Western Promenade. 01206 303067.
- Maldon, Promenade Park. 01621 856503.
- **C2** Beccles, Puddingmoor. 01502 713297.
- Fleggburgh, Broad Farm. (Summer only). 01493 369273.
- Halesworth, Dairy Hill. 01986 872720.

THEATRES

- **A1** Hunstanton, Princess Theatre, The Green. 01485 532252.
- King's Lynn, Corn Exchange, Tuesday Market Pl. 01553 764864.
- **A3** Cambridge, ADC Theatre, Park St. 01223 359547. Cambridge Drama Centre, Covent Garden, Mill Rd. 01223 578000. Concert Hall, West Rd. 01223 335184. Corn Exchange, Wheeler St. 01223 357851. The Junction, Clifton Rd. 01223 511511. Mumford Theatre, A.P.U. East Rd. 01223 352932.
- **A4** Chelmsford, Civic Theatre, Fairfield Rd. 01245 606505. Cramphorn Theatre, Fairfield Rd. 01245 606505. Old Court Theatre, Springfield Rd. 01245 263864/606505.
- Grays, Thameside Theatre, Orsett Rd. 01375 383961.
- Harlow, Playhouse, Playhouse Sq, The High. 01279 431945.
- Hornchurch, Queens Theatre, Billet La. 01708 443333.
- Ilford, Kenneth More Theatre, Oakfield Rd. 020 8553 4466.
- **B1** Cromer, Pavilion Theatre, The Pier Prom. 01263 512495.
- Holt, The Auden Theatre, Cromer Rd. 01263 713444.
- Sheringham, Little Theatre, 2 Station Rd. 01263 822347.
- **B2** Eye, Eye Theatre, Broad St. 01379 870519.
- Norwich, Maddermarket Theatre, St Johns Alley. 01603 620917. Norwich Arts Centre, Reeves Yard, St Benedicts St. 01603 660352. Playhouse, St George's St. 01603 612580. Studio Theatre, University of East Anglia, Earlham Rd. 01603 592272. Theatre Royal, Theatre St. 01603 630000. Whiffler Open Air Theatre, Castle Gardens (Summer programme). 01603 212136.

> Norwich Puppet Theatre, Whitefriars. One of only two puppet theatres in England, this regionally unique venue presents a regular programme of puppet plays by its own and visiting companies, plus children's puppet making workshops. For more information ring 01603 629921. Price code ⓓ. www.geocities.com/norwichpuppets

- Wingfield, Arts, off B1118. 01379 384505.
- **B3** Bury St. Edmunds, Theatre Royal, Westgate St. 01284 769505/755127.
- Colchester, Arts Centre, St. Mary-at-the-Walls, Church St. 01206 500900. Mercury Theatre, Balkerne Gate. 01206 573948.
- Ipswich, Corn Exchange, King St. 01473 433100/433133. Regent, St. Helen's St. 01473 433100/433555.
- Stowmarket, Regal Theatre, Ipswich St. 01449 612825.
- Sudbury, The Quay, Quay La. 01787 374745.
- **B4** Clacton-on-Sea, Princes Theatre, Town Hall, Station Rd. 01255 422958/423400.
- West Cliff Theatre, Tower Rd. 01255 433344.
- Westcliff-on-Sea, Cliffs Pavilion, Station

Map Ref: Grid square on page 2 map.   ✦ Birthday parties organised.

MAP REFS

B3 Rd. 01702 351135. **Palace Theatre**, 430 London Rd. 01702 342564/347816.

C2 **Great Yarmouth, Britannia Pier Theatre**, Marine Pde. 01493 842209. **Pavilion Theatre**, Pier Gdns, Gorleston. 01493 662832. **St. George's Theatre**, King St. 01493 858387.
Lowestoft, Marina Theatre, The Marina, 01502 573318. **Seagull Theatre**, Morton Rd. 01502 562863.
Southwold, Summer Theatre, St. Edmunds Hall, Cumberland Rd. 01502 722389/724441.

C3 **Felixstowe, Spa Pavilion**, Undercliff Rd. West. 01394 282126/283303.
Snape, Snape Concert Hall. 01728 687100.
Woodbridge, Riverside Theatre, Quayside. 01394 382174/382587.

TOURIST INFORMATION CENTRES

Cambridgeshire
Cambridge, 01223 322640
Ely, 01353 662062
Huntingdon, 01480 388588
St. Neots, 01480 388788

Essex
Birchanger Green, 01279 508656
Braintree, 01376 550066
Brentwood, 01277 200300
Chelmsford, 01245 283400
Clacton-on-Sea, 01255 423400
Colchester, 01206 282920
Harwich, 01255 506139
Maldon, 01621 856503
Redbridge, 020 8478 7145
Saffron Walden, 01799 510444
Southend-on-Sea, 01702 215120
Thurrock, 01708 863733
Waltham Abbey, 01992 652295

Norfolk
Attleborough, 01953 452404
Aylsham, 01263 733903

> **Broads Information**, Station Road, Hoveton/Wroxham. All you need to know about the Broads - places to visit and things to do, including boat trips, bike and canoe hire, children's events. 01603 782281.

Cromer, 01263 512497
Dereham, 01362 698992
Diss, 01379 650523
Downham Market, 01366 387440
Fakenham (seasonal), 01328 851981
Great Yarmouth (seasonal), 01493 842195

Hunstanton, 01485 532610
King's Lynn, 01553 763044
Norwich, 01603 666071
Swaffham (seasonal), 01760 722255
Wells-next-the-Sea (seasonal), 01328 710885
Wymondham, 01953 604721

Suffolk
Bury St. Edmunds, 01284 764667
Felixstowe, 01394 276770
Ipswich, 01473 258070
Lowestoft, 01502 533600
Newmarket, 01638 667200
Stowmarket, 01449 676800
Sudbury, 01787 881320
Woodbridge, 01394 382240

WATER FUN PARKS

Centres with some wonderful features, maybe flumes, wave machines or rapids!

A3 ♦ **Cambridge, Parkside Pools**, Gonville Pl 01223 446100.

A4 ♦ **Chelmsford, Riverside Ice and Leisure Centre**, Victoria Rd. 01245 615050.

B1 ♦ **Sheringham, Splash**, Weybourne Rd. 0126: 825675.

B2 ♦ **Norwich, Aquapark**, Drayton High Rd Hellesdon. 01603 788912.

♦ **Thetford, Waterworld**, Croxton Rd. 0184; 753110.

B3 ♦ **Bury St. Edmunds, LC**, Beetons Way. 0128 753496.

♦ **Colchester, Leisure World**, Cowdray Ave 01206 282000.

♦ **Ipswich, Crown Pools**, Crown St., is a grea day out for the whole family. Feature include a leisure pool with beach area competition pool, teaching pool, inflatab' fun sessions, sauna and a cafeteria. Profile Fitness Suite, which also offers yout classes. 01473 433655. (See Advert pac 22.)

♦ **Stowmarket, Mid Suffolk LC**, Gain: borough Rd. 01449 674980.

♦ **Sudbury, Kingfisher Leisure Pool**, Static Rd. 01787 375656.

B4 ♦ **Maldon, Blackwater**. 01621 851898.

C3 ♦ **Felixstowe, LC***, Undercliff Rd. Wes 01394 670411.

Map Ref: Grid square on page 2 map.   ♦ Birthday parties organised.

WATERSPORTS

Abbreviations: C: Canoeing, J: Jet Skiing, K: Kayaking, PB: Power Boating, S: Sailing, SD: Scuba Diving, T: Tubing, W: Windsurfing, WS: Waterskiing.

A1
East Winch, Pentney Lakes Leisure Park, Common Road. J, S, W, WS. 01760 338668.
King's Lynn, Surf 55, 125 Wootton Rd. W. 01553 679090.

A4
Basildon, Basildon Jet Ski Centre, Festival Leisure Park. 01268 270044.
✦ Chingford, Lee Valley Watersports Centre, C, S, W, WS. 020 8531 1129.
✦ Harlow, Outdoor Pursuits Centre, Burnt Mill La. C, K. (S. available at Broxbourne). 01279 432031.
✦ Ilford, Fairlop Waters Country Park, Forest Rd. C, W. 020 8501 1833.
Roydon, Roydon Mill Leisure Park, off B181, nr. Harlow. C, WS. 01279 792777
✦ South Ockenden, Grange Waters, Buckles La. C, S, SD, W. 01708 856422/855228. grangewater.@thurrock.gov.uk
Thurrock, Lakeside Diving & Watersports Centre, SD. 01708 860947.

B1
Brancaster Staithe, Sailcraft, The Boat Yard. PB, S, W. 01485 210236. www.sailcraft.co.uk

B2
✦ Norwich, Eagle Activity Centre, off
✦ Heigham St. C, K, RB. Whitlingham Little Broad Activity Centre, W. 01493 368129.

B3
Gosfield, Gosfield Lake Resort, Church Rd. WS. 01787 475043.
Ipswich, Suffolk Waters Country Park, Bramford. C, W. 01473 830191.
Stutton, Alton Water Sports Centre. S, W. 01473 328408.

B4
✦ Southend, Marine Activities Centre, Eastern Esplanade. C, J, PB, S, W. 01702 612770.
✦ Southminster, Bradwell Outdoor Education Centre, Bradwell Waterside. C, PB, S. 01621 776256.

C1
Hoveton, Norfolk Broads School of Sailing, The Rhond. S. 01603 783906.

C2
✦ Filby Broad, Activity Centre, C, K, PB, RB, S. 01493 368129.
Lowestoft, Wayman Outdoor & Leisure, Oulton Broad. C, W. 01502 564621.

Directory of Activities & Information

Europe's premier motorsport promoter *Spedeworth* INTERNATIONAL LTD

EXCITEMENT GUARANTEED

You'll find all the crashes and smashes you can handle at Foxhall and Swaffham Stadiums.

Big Bangers, Hot Rods, Stock Cars or even the stars of the future in their Ministox – the speed and action will knock your socks off!!!

We've got so many special events planned for 2002 including live music, special guest appearances, fireworks and big prizes to give away.

Call the HOTLINE on 09003 421 621 and get your family on the grid!
Call charged at 60p/min at all times

BANGERS
F1 STOCK CARS
HOT RODS
JUNIOR MINISTOX

SWAFFHAM STADIUM, NORFOLK
FOXHALL STADIUM, IPSWICH
www.stockcar.co.uk

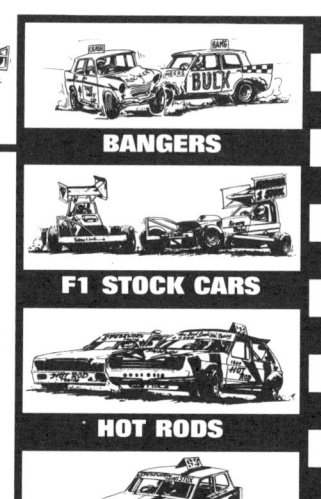

Boat & Train Trips

MAP REFS	PRICE CODES

Have a change from the car. Try a train or a boat trip.

BOAT TRIPS

A1 **from Hunstanton.** Seal trips, fishing trips and rides in a WWII ex-army DUKW to view the coastline or visit the wreck of "Sheraton". 07831 321799.

A3 **from Cambridge.** Chauffeur Punts operate from Newnham Mill Pond, The Granta Inn. Tours of "The Backs" from 45 mins-1 hour and trips to Granchester "through the meadows". 01223 301845. www.puntingincambridge.com

A4 Schools **from Broxbourne.** Enjoy cruising the River Lee on a choice of three trip boats, "Lady of Lee Valley", "Adventuress" and the smaller "Soliloquy". These traditional canal cruisers offer public trips and private charters from Easter to Dec, Suns, Bank Hols and school Summer hols. Educational cruises available. 01992 466111. www.rivercruises.co.uk

from Tilbury. Tilbury-Gravesend Ferry, Fort Road, boarding at Tilbury riverside, leaves at regular intervals daily (except Suns and Bank Hols) and crosses the River Thames at a point where all manner of craft can be spotted. 01474 566220.

B1 Schools **from Morston Quay,** take a trip to see the seals and a wealth of bird life at Blakeney Point nature reserve. 01263 740038; 740505; 740753 & 740791.

B2 Schools Open all year **from Norwich.** A variety of trips with live commentary, ranging from half an hour to over three hours, from Elm Hill Quay, Norwich Station Quay and Griffin Lane, Thorpe St Andrew. 01603 701701.

B4 **from Flatford.** You can take 1/2 hour trips from Flatford Lock in a 12 seater, pollution free, electric launch. Also available for charter. Easter-mid Oct, Suns & Bank Hols (also Weds in Aug). 01206 392656/393680.

Schools **from Little Baddow.** Enjoy lovely, peaceful rural cruising. Charter hire for groups. Apr to Oct. 01245 225520.

from Southend-on-Sea. There are regular services from Southend Pier. 0141 243 2224. www.waverleyexcursions.co.uk.

C1 **from Horning.** The Mississippi Paddle Boat takes you on a luxury trip on the Norfolk Broads. Public trips daily, with bar and commentary. Private hire available. 01692 630262

Schools **from How Hill,** Ludham, travel through the reeds and fens of this tranquil reserve on the Edwardian-style "Electric Eel". Trip lasts 50 minutes, including short walk to bird hide. Departs How Hill Staithe. Booking advisable as boat takes maximum 8 people. 01692 678763. (See Toad Hole Cottage in "Free Places" chapter.)

Schools **from Wroxham.** Relaxing Broadland tours, in traditional style and double-decker boats. (Combine with a nostalgic steam journey on the Bure Valley Railway.) Educational discovery trips available to include activities. 01603 782207.

C2 **from Great Yarmouth,** daily sea trips run to Scroby sands, one mile offshore from the beach at Britannia Pier. See the seals basking on the sands and enjoy live commentary on the history of this famous resort. 01493 602724.

Schools **from Oulton Broad** (near Lowestoft). Broad and river cruises including day trips 01502 574903/07703 854007.

C3 **from Orford.** You can cruise from Orford to Aldeburgh passing Havergate Island famous for avocets, and the Heritage Coast. Available all year. 07831 698396.

Schools **from Orford.** 1 hour trips round Havergate Island RSPB reserve in an open launch Apr-Oct. Trips through the Winter by arrangement. 01394 450844.

Schools **from Waldringfield.** Cruise on the picturesque River Deben. Book in advance. 0147 736260.

Price Codes for a family of four: **(A)**: less than £5 **(B)**: £5-£10 **(C)**: £10-£15 **(D)**: £15-£20 **(E)**: £20-£30 **(G)**: £30-£50 **(H)**: Over £50 **(F)**: Free
Map Ref: Grid square on Page 2 Map   Schools: Facilities available   ● Birthday parties

Boat & Train Trips

TRAIN TRIPS

Central Trains services provide travel to over 250 destinations including major cities such as Nottingham, Leicester, Birmingham, Manchester, Liverpool and Cambridge. There are good connections to services covering the rest of the country too so that reaching destinations further afield becomes that little bit easier. In addition the trains call at rural retreats and historic market towns such as Warwick, Newark and Shrewsbury providing convenient travel for a memorable day out. Whether you are visiting friends or family, exploring a new city or a new attraction, indulging in some shopping or travelling to the airport, you can rest assured that Central Trains aims to provide all its customers with a fast and pleasant journey avoiding the hassles of traffic jams and parking. Go by train! Contact your local station or visit the website for more information. www.centraltrains.co.uk (See Advert inside front cover.)

A3 — Ⓑ Schools — **Audley End Railway**, Audley End. Close to English Heritage property Audley End House and Park (see "Historic Sites" chapter), is a steam railway which takes you for a ride through picturesque woods. Open 23rd Mar-last Sun in Oct, weekends and Bank Hols, and daily in school hols, from 2pm. Santa Specials in Dec. 01799 541354. www.audley-end-railway.co.uk

B1 — Ⓓ Schools 🎂 — **Bure Valley Railway**, Aylsham. Take a nine-mile trip from Aylsham to Wroxham along Norfolk's longest narrow gauge railway. The Boat Train connects with cruises on the Broads - inclusive fares available. Open 9.30am-5.30pm, Mar-Oct. Phone for timetable information. Santa Specials during Dec (pre booking required). Phone 01263 733858. www.bvrw.co.uk Combines with "Huff" and "Puff" cycle trail, a nine-mile traffic free trail alongside train track. Cycles available for hire at both Aylsham and Wroxham stations. (01263 732935 for cycle hire only.)

Ⓓ Schools Open all year 🎂 — **North Norfolk Railway**, The Station, **Sheringham**. Travel back in time along the scenic North Norfolk coastline on a 5-mile journey by steam train between the stations of Sheringham, Weybourne and Holt. Station open daily, 9.30am-5.30pm. Train trips, Sat, Sun, Tues-Thurs, Mar-May and daily Jun-mid Sept, weekends only, mid Sept-Feb. Mince Pie Specials, 26th Dec-1st Jan. 01263 820800.

Ⓓ Schools — **Wells and Walsingham Light Railway**, Stiffkey Road, **Wells-next-the-Sea**. Ride the longest 10¹/₄" narrow gauge steam railway in the world on the unique Garratt locomotive 'Norfolk Hero', built especially for this line. The timetabled service between the seaside and harbour town of Wells to the picturesque pilgrimage centre of Walsingham is a scenic journey through lovely countryside, with halts at Warham St Mary and Wighton. The regular service gives ample time to explore Walsingham and its famous shrine before catching the train back. The main station at Wells has a charming restored signal box where refreshments and souvenirs are available. Open daily, Good Fri-31st Oct. Call the talking timetable 01328 710631, or 01328 711630 for further details. (See Advert page 28.)

Ⓐ Schools — **Wells Harbour Railway**, Wells-next-the-Sea. Head for the beach on board Edmund or Densil, the first narrow gauge steam and diesel railway engines to operate a scheduled passenger service. Open Easter-end Sept, 10.30am-5pm (late trains at busy periods). 01328 710964. www.wellsharbourrailway.com

32 — **Mid-Norfolk Railway**, Station Road, **Dereham**. An 11-mile journey, through rural mid-Norfolk, between Wymondham, Dereham and North Elmham. Santa Specials during Dec. Ring for further timetable information. 01362 690633.

33 — Ⓒ Schools — **Colne Valley Railway**, Castle Hedingham, offers a programme of "Steam Days" and special events throughout the year when rides are available. Phone for free timetable of open times and events. (See "Historic Sites" chapter.) 01787 461174. www.cvr.org.uk

---

Price Codes for a family of four: Ⓐ: less than £5   Ⓑ: £5-£10   Ⓒ: £10-£15   Ⓓ: £15-£20   Ⓔ: £20-£30   Ⓖ: £30-£50   Ⓗ: Over £50   Ⓕ: Free
Map Ref: Grid square on Page 2 Map   Schools: Facilities available   🎂 Birthday parties

MAP REFS	PRICE CODES		
B3	Ⓑ / Ⓒ Schools Open all year	**East Anglian Railway Museum,** Chappel, near Colchester, provides an opportunity to enjoy a steam train ride on "Steam Days". (See "Historic Sites" chapter.)
B4	Ⓒ Schools	**Mangapps Farm Railway Museum,** Burnham-on-Crouch, offers rides on a three-quarters of a mile track on "Steam Days". (See "Historic Sites" chapter.)
	Ⓑ Open all year	**Southend Pier Railway,** Southend-on-Sea, provides an exhilarating ride, departing at regular intervals along the longest pleasure pier in the world. Open 8am-4pm, 6pm weekends in Winter, 8am-9pm, 10pm weekends in Summer. Closed 25th Dec. 01702 215620.
	Ⓒ	**The New Walton Pier Company,** Walton-on-the-Naze. Take a train ride to the end of the pier. Open end Mar-end Sept, daily from Whitsun. (See "Theme Parks & Play Parks" chapter.)

WELLS & WALSINGHAM LIGHT RAILWAY
Wells Next-The-Sea, North Norfolk

Visit the longest 10¼" Narrow Gauge Steam Railway in the world.

A great adventure for all the family in the delightful countryside of the North Norfolk Coast.

Open 7 Days a week
from Good Friday to 31st October.
Talking Timetable: 01328 710631

One of Britain's Great Little Railways

tots to teens furniture barn

Specialist Makers and Retailers

We offer an extensive selection of nursery, bedroom and playroom furniture for children, to suit all budgets and tastes.
Our family friendly showroom is located on a 'farm' with free parking, toys and videos.

Just 5 minutes from Jct. 6 - A1
Hertford 8 minutes (A10)

Telephone for details/map:
07957-870043
email: info@totstoteensfurniture.co.uk
www.totstoteensfurniture.co.uk

Price Codes for a family of four: Ⓐ: less than £5 Ⓑ: £5-£10 Ⓒ: £10-£15 Ⓓ: £15-£20 Ⓔ: £20-£30 Ⓖ: £30-£50 Ⓗ: Over £50 Ⓕ: Free
Map Ref: Grid square on Page 2 Map   Schools: Facilities available   ● Birthday parties

BRING YOUR FAMILY TO MEET OURS!

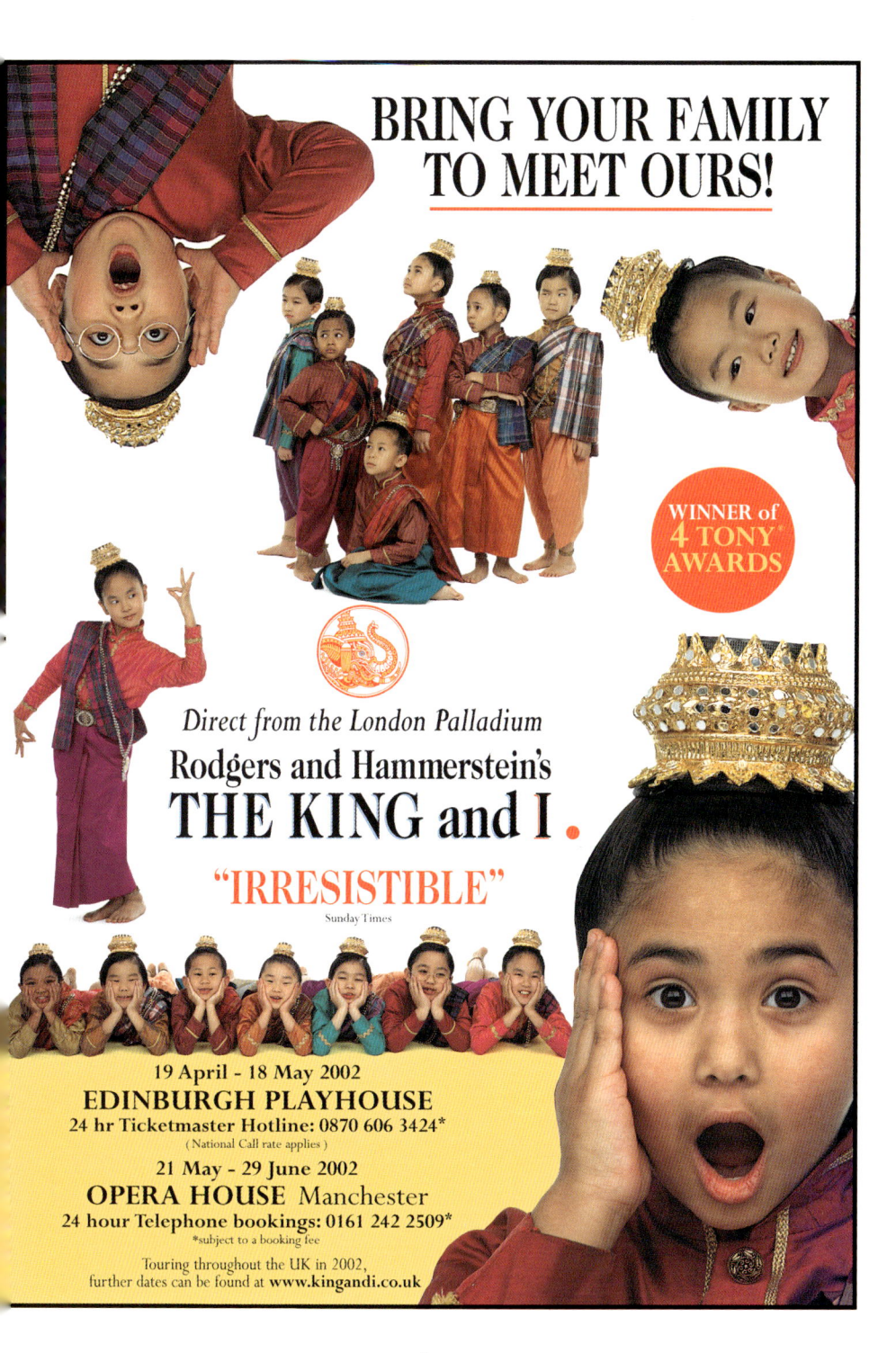

WINNER of 4 TONY AWARDS

Direct from the London Palladium

Rodgers and Hammerstein's
THE KING and I

"IRRESISTIBLE"
Sunday Times

19 April - 18 May 2002
EDINBURGH PLAYHOUSE
24 hr Ticketmaster Hotline: 0870 606 3424*
(National Call rate applies)

21 May - 29 June 2002
OPERA HOUSE Manchester
24 hour Telephone bookings: 0161 242 2509*
*subject to a booking fee

Touring throughout the UK in 2002,
further dates can be found at www.kingandi.co.uk

HMS BELFAST

Now FREE for children under 16

Visit HMS *Belfast* and find out what it was really like on the open sea.
A tour of this huge and complex warship will take you from HMS *Belfast's* Quarterdeck all the way down through nine decks to her massive Boiler and Engine Rooms, well below the ship's waterline.

HMS *Belfast*, Morgans Lane, Tooley Street, London SE1 2JH
Telephone 020 7940 6300.   www.iwm.org.uk

Why not hold your child's birthday party on board? Call 020 7940 6320 for details

THE CUTTY SARK TRUST — GREENWICH

See what life was really like for the sailors!
New children's displays
Award winning education program
Visitors Shop

Cutty Sark, King William Walk,
Greenwich London SE10 9HT
Tel: 020 8858 3445   Fax: 020 8853 3589
info@cuttysark.org.uk   www.cuttysark.org.uk

ROYAL BOTANIC GARDENS KEW

Kew Gardens

discover your planet

24hr information   020 8332 5655   www.kew.org

Let's Visit London

LONDON

PRICE CODES

Ⓑ Cutty Sark, King William Walk, Greenwich, now 133 years old, was built in 1869 on the River Clyde in Scotland. Built to be a very fast ship of the Victorian era, she carried tea from China and years later, wool from Australia. Visit her now to see what life was like for the men who sailed on her. Look at the contrast between the sailors' cabins on the main deck and the officers' cabins and the Master's Saloon! There are new displays on board for children and in the lower hold you can try your hand at knot tying and lifting heavy weights by pulling on lines. An award winning educational program enables children to become Victorian sailors for a day and there is good pre-visit material for teachers. Lots to see and do here to interest and fascinate all the family. Open daily, 10am-5pm. Closed 24th-26th Dec. 020 8858 3445. www.cuttysark.org.uk (See Advert page ii.)

Schools Open all year

Ⓒ HMS Belfast, off Morgans Lane, Tooley Street, is just a short walk from Tower Bridge. This unique floating exhibit will offer an enthralling voyage of discovery for both you and your children. HMS Belfast is Europe's only surviving big gun armoured warship to have seen action in the Second World War. Explore all nine decks of this historic warship, from the Quarterdeck, up to the Captain's Bridge, into the Gun Turrets and down into the Boiler and Engine Rooms, way below the ship's waterline. Experience what it was like to be a member of the ship's company on board HMS Belfast during the Second World War by visiting the Artic Messdecks, Sick Bay, Dental Surgery, Ship's Galley and Punishment Cells. Children will love the adventure here, but they must be supervised at all times and care should be taken when negotiating the ladders leading from deck to deck. Not suitable for infants. Two decks accessible to disabled visitors. School facilities: contact the Education Officer Michelle Ruddenklau directly on 020 7940 6323. Birthday parties available on board. Please call 020 7940 6320 for an information pack. Open daily except for the Christmas period 24th-26th Dec. Summer: 10am-6pm (last admission 5.15pm); Winter: 10am-5pm (last admission 4.15pm). Entrance is free for children under 16. 020 7940 6300. www.iwm.org.uk (See Advert page ii.)

Schools Open all year

↔ *Tower Hill London Bridge*

Ⓖ Chelsea World Of Sport, Chelsea Village, Fulham Road, provides a lively and fun opportunity to explore a variety of sports and many aspects of sports science from nutrition to physiology as well as celebrating the history of achievements of Chelsea Football Club. Football plays an important part among the interactive displays. In the 'Ball Control' area, you enter a 'pitch' and with help from a qualified coach can attempt to dribble the ball around a series of defenders as quickly as possible before trying to beat the keeper with a shot at the goal. 'Throw In' allows a participant to throw a ball into play and test their strength and accuracy of their shots. 'Get Off The Blocks' offers you the chance to race against a top sprinter while 'Virtual Volleyball' monitors the player's movements and projects graphic images of them onto a screen. 'Rockface Challenge' gives you the opportunity to climb a mountain without ever having to leave Chelsea. You can also learn about how the body works during different sporting activities and the effect on the human anatomy of pushing it to the limit. There is information on sports nutrition and how the body uses various different types of food. Special facilities for schools include a teacher's resource room, teacher training days and curriculum linked programmes. Open Mon-Fri, 10am-6pm, Sat & Sun, 9am-6pm. Match days, club members only, 9am-12noon. 020 7915 2222 www.chelseaworldofsport.com (See Advert page xii.)

Schools Open all year

↔ *Fulham Broadway*

Ⓒ Kew Gardens. Explore Kew's spectacular gardens and see the world! You can go on a journey from jungle to desert in the magnificent glasshouses. Find the giant waterlily or watch piranhas swimming through the Marine Display in the Palm House. Step back thousands of years and follow the sights, scents and sounds of plant life through time in the exciting Evolution House. Visit the Museum with the fascinating interactive exhibition Plants+People, which highlights the importance of plants to mankind. Find the Minka house and the Pagoda, or let your senses guide you in the Secluded Garden. Hop on the Kew Explorer bus for a fun way to tour round the gardens. Children's activities, themed displays and seasonal festivals are held throughout the year. Fantastic places to eat and shop. Easy to reach on the district line tube, by train or car. Open daily from 9.30am-5.30pm,

Schools Open all year

Price Codes for a family of four: Ⓐ: less than £5 Ⓑ: £5-£10 Ⓒ: £10-£15 Ⓓ: £15-£20 Ⓔ: £20-£30 Ⓖ: £30-£50 Ⓗ:- Over £50 Ⓕ: Free
Schools: Range of educational opportunities available. 🎈 Birthday parties organised. ↔ Nearest tube station.

LONDON BUTTERFLY HOUSE
AT
SYON PARK
100's OF FREE FLYING BUTTERFLIES IN AN INDOOR TROPICAL GARDEN. SEPARATE DISPLAYS OF ANTS, INSECTS & SPIDERS
ALWAYS AN ADVENTURE - WHATEVER THE WEATHER!
OPEN DAILY
TELEPHONE TO CONFIRM
TIMES & PRICES
SYON PARK, BRENTFORD, MIDDX. TEL: 0208 - 560 - 7272
AMPLE FREE CAR PARKING
http://www.butterflies.org.uk/

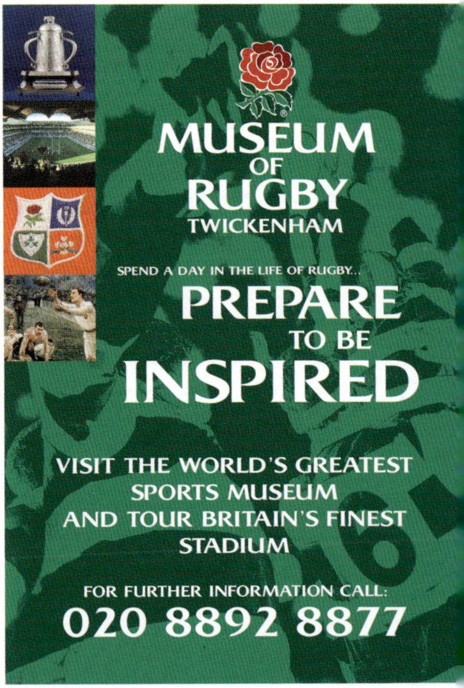
MUSEUM
OF
RUGBY
TWICKENHAM
SPEND A DAY IN THE LIFE OF RUGBY...
PREPARE
TO BE
INSPIRED
VISIT THE WORLD'S GREATEST SPORTS MUSEUM AND TOUR BRITAIN'S FINEST STADIUM
FOR FURTHER INFORMATION CALL:
020 8892 8877

Take an
underwater
nature trail...
LONDON
AQUARIUM
Witness the frantic feeding time in the piranha display...
Find the most dangerous fish in the world in the Indian Ocean...
For further information:
020 7967 8000
www.londonaquarium.co.uk
Westminster, Waterloo
Waterloo, Waterloo Eas

PRICE CODES

↔ 3.45pm in Winter, except 25th Dec and 1st Jan. Children under 17 are admitted free. 24 hour
Kew Gardens   information line: 020 8332 5655. www.kew.org.uk (See Advert page ii.)

Ⓔ **The London Aquarium,** County Hall, Westminster Bridge Road, is one of Europe's largest
Schools   displays of aquatic life with over 350 species in over 50 displays, ranging from the mystical seahorse
Open all   to the deadly stonefish. The huge pacific display is home to a variety of jacks, stingrays and eight
year   sharks, including the only zebra shark in the country. Witness the spectacular Atlantic feed where
a team of divers hand feed six foot long conger eels, rays and British sharks. The friendly rays can't
resist popping up to the surface to say hello and to get stroked by the visitors. The rainforest feed
incorporates a frenzied piranha feed with the amazing marksmanship of the archerfish. There is a
range of education tours and literature available to enhance a visit. Open daily 10am-6pm, last
↔ admission 5pm. Closed Christmas Day. 0207 967 8000 www.londonaquarium.co.uk
Waterloo or
Westminster   (See Advert page iv.)

Ⓒ/Ⓓ **The London Butterfly House,** Syon Park, Brentford. Many varied and colourful butterflies
Schools   from all over the world are free to fly around as you walk through the large greenhouse. Lushly
Open all   planted with flowering shrubs and tropical plants, it provides the right conditions for butterflies to
year   fly, court, lay eggs, feed and bask in the sunlight. See some strange and wonderful looking
💡   caterpillars and a remarkable leaf-cutter ant colony! Enjoy the new Exotic Bird Aviary and a separate
↔ area displaying spiders, scorpions and weird stick insects. Open daily except Christmas, 10am-5pm,
Gunnersbury   3.30pm in Winter. 0208 560 7272. www.butterflies.org.uk (See Advert page iv.)

Ⓒ **London's Transport Museum,** Covent Garden Piazza, using imaginative and dynamic
Schools   displays, takes you on a fascinating journey through time and recounts the story of the interaction
Open all   between transport, the capital and its people from 1800 to the present day. Look out for the under
year   5s funbus, try the bus and tube simulators, meet characters from the past, see models and working
displays and get interactive in the many "KidZones". More fun learning than you would have thought
possible! Good educational material and lots of special holiday activities. There is now free admission
for children under 16. Open daily, 10am-6pm, but 11am-6pm on Fridays. Last admission 5.15pm. Closed
↔ 24th-26th Dec. 020 7565 7299 for recorded information. Education service: 020 7379 6344.
Covent Garden   www.ltmuseum.co.uk (See Advert page vi.)

Ⓓ **Museum of Rugby and Twickenham Stadium Tour,** Rugby Road, Twickenham.
Schools   Prepare to be inspired spending a day in the life of rugby! From the moment you pass through the
Open all   authentic Twickenham turnstile at the Museum of Rugby, you'll be immersed in a world of Rugby
year   history. Enjoy some of the finest and most extensive collection of rugby memorabilia in the world.
💡   Let interactive touch-screen computers, video footage and period set pieces take you on a journey
through the history of the game. Also operating from the Museum are tours of the rugby stadium.
Expert tour guides will take you on an awe-inspiring journey through the home of England rugby. Walk
alongside the hallowed turf, visit England's dressing room and experience the excitement of match
day as you enter the stadium through the players' tunnel. Open daily, Tues-Sat & Bank Hols 10am-
5pm, Sun 11-5pm. Match days: open to match ticket holders only. Closed Mons, 24th-27th Dec and
Good Fri. 020 8892 8877. www.rfu.com (See Advert page iv.)

Ⓕ **The National Maritime Museum,** Maritime Greenwich World Heritage Site. Housed
Schools   within a breathtaking architectural space, the Museum tells the story of the sea in a radical new way.
Open all   A flashing lighthouse optic and a huge revolving propeller from a modern frigate sets the scene at
year   the entrance to remind you of the scale of the sea. The Museum not only looks back at history but
also challenges the future in dramatic and imaginative displays, many of them interactive. Steer
Viking boats and Seacat ferries, load cargoes and discover amazing curiosities plucked from the
ocean. In the 'Future of the Sea' gallery, a huge sphere and audio-visual effects illuminate the water
cycle which is the very building block of life on earth. From March 2002, in the new 'Making Waves'
gallery, a wave tank gives a vivid demonstration of how oceans affect all life on the planet and you
can generate twisting currents, vortexes and whirlpools. The 'Search Station' computer facility gives
access to even more treasures and 'New Visions of the Sea' showcases creative interpretations of

Price Codes for a family of four: Ⓐ: less than £5   Ⓑ: £5-£10   Ⓒ: £10-£15   Ⓓ: £15-£20   Ⓔ: £20-£30   Ⓖ: £30-£50   Ⓗ:- Over £50   Ⓕ: Free
Schools: Range of educational opportunities available.   ● Birthday parties organised.   ↔ Nearest tube station.

BE MOVED

Be inspired by the wonders of London's transport system.

Be amazed by hands-on exhibits, simulators and fun activities.

Be moved by a great day out.

www.ltmuseum.co.uk
(020) 7565 7299

kids go FREE

London's Transport Museum
Covent Garden Piazza

River Red Rover Ticket

Unlimited daily river travel between Westminster, Waterloo, Tower & Greenwich for just

£8 for adults
£4 for childrens
£21 for family tickets

Telephone : 02077 400 400

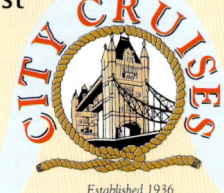

CITY CRUISES
Established 1936

the limitless possibilities of the sea. Visit also the Royal Observatory and the Queen's House, both within the Heritage Site. Open daily 10am-5pm. Closed 24th-26th Dec. Charges for special exhibitions only. 020 8312 6608 (Bookings); 020 88584422. www.nmm.ac.uk (See Advert page xiv).

(F) Schools Open all year

The Natural History Museum, Cromwell Road, houses an amazing world of natural treasures and provides an opportunity to explore the Earth and its life, both past and present. Perennial favourites include 'Dinosaurs', with life-sized robotic models, 'The Power Within' with its 'Earthquake Experience' and 'Human Biology' offering scores of interactive experiences. Don't miss special exhibitions: 'Predators' featuring a robotic shark, spider and chameleon (until 6th May), 'BG Wildlife Photographer of the Year' (until 11th Mar), 'Turbulent Landscapes' (19th Apr-15th Sept) and 'Dinobirds: The Feathered Dinosaurs of China' (18th Jul-5th May 2003). Open Mon-Sat 10am-5.50pm* (*last admission 5.30pm), Sun 11am-5.50pm.* Closed 24th-26th Dec. Admission is free. Call for details of special exhibition prices 020 7942 5000 or visit the website: www.nhm.ac.uk (See Advert page xii)

↔ South Kensington

Let's take a trip

on a bus . . .

(G) Open all year

The Original Tour, London Sightseeing Bus Tours. An open top bus ride is a wonderful way to travel and introduce children to the splendid sights of London. The Original Tour offer an excellent service, with over 90 stops to hop-on and off, six tour routes, an entertaining commentary available on board all of the buses, and, a famous 'Kids Club'. Children are both entertained and educated by the special commentary designed for children, as magical stories about London unfold with tales from Roman times until the present day. Listen out for the ghostly 'Spirit of London'. The service runs frequently, seven days a week, from a variety of easily accessed stops. Times vary seasonally for each route. To celebrate over 50 years of sightseeing The Original Tour are now giving every customer a free Thames River Cruise! For more information or to enjoy a special discount call 020 8877 1722 and quote 'Let's Go special offer', or visit the website: www.theoriginaltour.com (See Advert page viii).

on the canal . . .

©/(G) Schools Open all year

Canal Waterbus will enable you to see a side of London that you never knew existed. Take a boat trip along the Regents Canal, through the green and leafy Regents Park and the dark mysterious Maida Hill Tunnel. Boats leave from Camden Lock, with its unique atmosphere and unusual shopping, and/or Little Venice, with its island, ducks and boats. You can stop off at London Zoo to visit the animals via a special canal gate. Excellent educational resources and special group rates. Trips run daily Apr-Oct, weekends only Nov-Mar. Information: 020 7482 2660. Bookings: 020 7482 2550.

↔ Camden Town

on the River Thames . . .

(E) Open all year

On the River Thames with City Cruises. Add some excitement for the children, a new perspective for everyone and get excellent value by seeing some of London's best sights from the River Thames aboard a City Cruises luxury river-liner using a brand new River Red Rover ticket! You can also now travel as far as Greenwich to see the Cutty Sark. For just £8 for an adult ticket, £4 for a child, you can use a hop-on hop-off service between the major destination piers on the River! From Westminster Pier services run, every 20 minutes to Tower Pier, and, every 40 minutes to Greenwich via Waterloo and Tower Pier. Your River Red Rover will give you unlimited daily travel between these piers. Admire the Houses of Parliament and Big Ben, see St Paul's Cathedral, look out for the Tate Modern, see if you can spot Shakespeare's Globe. Lots to see from these super boats with cafe style facilities and a capacity of 520 seats which operate every day of the year. 02077 400 400. www.citycruises.com (See Advert page vi).

↔ Waterloo, Westminster, Tower Hill

Price Codes for a family of four: (A): less than £5 (B): £5-£10 (C): £10-£15 (D): £15-£20 (E): £20-£30 (G): £30-£50 (H):- Over £50 (F): Free
Schools: Range of educational opportunities available. ● Birthday parties organised. ↔ Nearest tube station.

The ORIGINAL SIGHTSEEING TOUR of LONDON by OPEN-TOP BUS

The Original Tour — London Sightseeing
Includes FREE RIVER CRUISE

Insist on 'The Original'. Live English speaking guides and seven language commentaries.

KIDS CLUB

Exclusive 'Kids Club' includes commentary especially for children and free activity packs

www.theoriginaltour.com
Tel: 020 8877 1722

Telephone booking discount – quote LGWC

ATTENTION ALL PARENTS
MUSIC • SINGING • DANCING

Jo Jingles is the leading pre-school music club in the UK with classes in over 150 centres, and we are growing daily

NURSERY RHYMES, SONGS, MUSICAL INSTRUMENT PLAYING, FUN SESSIONS WITH AN EDUCATIONAL SLANT, INTERACTIVE PROGRAMMES

For further details on Jo Jingles classes in your area, or setting up a business running Jo Jingles classes, please call:

01494 676575
quoting 'Let's Go 02'

headoffice@jojingles.co.uk
www.jojingles.co.uk

THE MUSIC & MOVEMENT EXPERIENCE

CATS

CATS 21st ANNIVERSARY YEAR

A MEMORY THAT WILL LAST FOREVER

Monday to Saturday evenings 7.30pm • Tuesday and Saturday matinees 3.00pm
FOR SHOW TICKETS AND INFORMATION ON SATURDAY KIDS' CLUB
CALL 020 7405 0072
NEW LONDON THEATRE, DRURY LANE, LONDON WC2

PRICE CODES

LONDON

Let's Play

Jo Jingles, a leading pre-school music and singing club with an educational slant, runs exciting and stimulating music and movement classes for pre-school children at venues all over the country. A fun introduction to music, singing and movement, is offered, using action songs, musical instruments, dancing and educational themes in a stimulating and happy environment. Weekly classes for 1-2 year olds, 2-3 year olds, 3-5 year olds and 5-7 year olds are available. For details of classes in your area, call 01494 676255. Email: headoffice@jojingles.co.uk www.jojingles.co.uk (See Advert page viii.)

Schools Open all year
↔ *Gunnersbury*

Snakes and Ladders, Syon Park, Brentford, is well signposted from Syon Park or can be accessed via 237 or 267 bus from Kew Bridge BR or Gunnersbury Underground Station. Children can find action packed fun whatever the weather. They can let off steam in the giant supervised indoor main playframe, intermediate 2-5s area or toddlers area or use the outdoor adventure playground when the sun shines. A mini motor bike circuit provides an exciting additional activity. Meanwhile parents can relax in the cafe overlooking the playframe. Open daily 10am-6pm. Last admission 5.15pm. All children must wear socks. 020 8847 0946.

Let's Go to a Café

Schools Open all year
↔ *Golders Green*

The Clay Cafe, 8-10 Monkville Parade, Finchley Road, Temple Fortune, is a hub of cuisine and entertainment that positively welcomes families with children of all ages. This intriguing combination of a full service bistro style restaurant plus a paint-it-yourself ceramic studio offers a fresh and innovative approach to providing creative relaxation for both adults and children alike. Choose from over 200 pieces of pottery (dinnerware, vases, animals etc) and a qualified Art Technician will assist you in creating a unique masterpiece! Glass painting, mosaicing and T-shirt painting are also on offer. Open Sun-Fri 11am-10pm, Sat 10am-11pm. Prices vary. 020 8905 5353. www.theclaycafe.co.uk

Schools Open all year
↔ *Piccadilly*

The Rainforest Cafe, 20 Shaftesbury Avenue, Piccadilly Circus, brings the sights, sounds and smells of a tropical rainforest into a 340-seat restaurant spanning three floors. Tour guides lead adventurers to their tables and orders are taken by experienced Safari guides. A range of tasty sounding foods are on offer with wonderfully exciting names and whilst choosing from the exotic menu, enjoy the special effects which include tropical rain showers, thunder and lightning storms, cascading waterfalls, rainforest mists and the cacophony of wildlife noises. Look out for the myriads of tropical fish, the chattering gorillas, trumpeting elephants, slithering boa and life-sized crocodile! Reservations possible with the exception of weekends and school holidays. Open Mon-Fri from 12 noon, weekends & holidays open from 11.30am. 020 7434 3111. www.therainforestcafe.co.uk (See Advert page x)

Let's Go to the Theatre

Ⓗ *Schools Open all year*
↔ *Covent Garden*

CATS, New London Theatre, Drury Lane, is the longest-running musical in British theatre history! Combining the exhilarating music of Andrew Lloyd Webber, spellbinding tales from TS Eliot's 'Old Possum's Book of Practical Cats' and some of the most exciting choreography ever seen on stage, CATS really is a memory that will last forever. You can also now experience another dimension to the magical musical world of CATS - A twice a month Saturday Kids Club gives children a unique opportunity to enter into the world of theatre. The 3 hour experience includes face-painting, backstage tour, drama workshops, snack lunch and the opportunity to meet a cast member. Appropriate for ages 8-15, from 11.30am - 2.30pm. For further information on the Kids Club and for show tickets call the box office on 020 7405 0072. Education resource pack and workshop information available on request for school groups, please contact the Education Dept. on 020 7400 5005. Group bookings 020 7400 5007 www.catsthemusical.com (See Advert page viii.)

Ⓗ *Open all year*

My Fair Lady, Theatre Royal Drury Lane, Catherine Street. This world famous musical tells the story of Henry Higgins, an opinionated linguistics professor, who makes a wager with a colleague that within six months he can transform a cockney flower seller, Eliza Doolittle, into a lady who can

Price Codes for a family of four: Ⓐ: less than £5 Ⓑ: £5-£10 Ⓒ: £10-£15 Ⓓ: £15-£20 Ⓔ: £20-£30 Ⓖ: £30-£50 Ⓗ: Over £50 Ⓕ: Free
Schools: Range of educational opportunities available.   Birthday parties organised.   ↔ Nearest tube station.

Rainforest Cafe

A WILD PLACE TO SHOP AND EAT®

"Your Adventure Is About To Begin"

Feast from our generous and exotic menu.
Wonder at the sights and sounds of the rainforest.

Telephone: 020 7434 3111

Shaftesbury Avenue, Piccadilly Circus, London Open from 12 noon daily www.therainforestcafe.co

---

Cut out this voucher and bring it with you to receive a

Free Smoothie or Dessert
with every main course ordered by your party

Please present to your safari guide when seated. Cannot be used in conjunction with any other o

Ref: Let's Go with the Children

PRICE CODES

↔ Covent Garden

take her place in high society. Bookings: 020 7494 5000. Group bookings: 020 7494 5454. www.myfairladythemusical.com

Ⓗ Open all year

The Lion King, Lyceum Theatre, Wellington Street. One of the most successful Disney films in history, stunningly recreated on stage, is a thrilling and original musical which brings a rich sense of Africa to the stage through a medley of exotic sights and sounds. The show opens in the well loved Disney setting of 'Pride Rock' where 'Simba' the new lion cub is presented to a magical parade of Safari animals. One cannot fail to appreciate the inspiration that allows the giraffes to strut, the birds to swoop and the gazelles to bound. This initial spectacle is breathtaking as the entire savannah comes to life. Wonder at the creativity of the set as the sun rises, savannah plains sway, cattle stampede, drought takes hold and starry skies give up their secrets. Huge variety is offered in the musical score ranging from pulsating African rhythms to contemporary rock. Tim Rice and Elton John's Oscar winning work is unforgettable. A show not to be missed. Ticket hotline 0870 243 9000,

↔ Covent Garden

or for group bookings 020 7957 4070. (See Advert below)

Ⓗ Schools Open all year

Les Misérables, Palace Theatre, Shaftesbury Avenue, The world's most popular musical, based on Victor Hugo's great novel, an epic tale of passion and destruction, against the background of a nation in the grip of revolutionary turmoil. To book tickets call the box office on 020 7434 0909. Education resource pack available on request, please contact the Education Dept. on 020 7494 1670.

↔ Piccadilly

Group bookings 020 7494 1671. www.lesmis.com

Ⓗ Open all year

The Phantom Of The Opera, Her Majesty's Theatre, Haymarket. With some of the most lavish sets, costumes and special effects ever to have been created for the stage, this haunting musical traces the tragic love story of a beautiful opera singer and a young composer shamed by his physical appearance into a shadowy existence beneath the majestic Paris Opera House. Bookings: 020

↔ Piccadilly

7494 5400. Group bookings: 020 7494 5454. www.thephantomoftheopera.com

LONDON

'FAMILY ENTERTAINMENT AT ITS BEST'
DAILY TELEGRAPH

DISNEY PRESENTS

THE LION KING

THE Nº 1 SHOW IN LONDON

MATINEES : SUNDAY AT 3PM,
WEDNESDAY AND SATURDAY AT 2PM,
TICKETS FROM £17.50

CALL 'THE LION KING' HOTLINE :
0870 243 9000

LYCEUM THEATRE
A CLEARCHANNEL ENTERTAINMENT VENUE • WELLINGTON STREET, LONDON WC2
© DISNEY

OPEN 7 DAYS A WEEK

FREE ADMISSION

Monday-Saturday 10.00-17.50,
Sunday 11.00-17.50.
Cromwell Road, London SW7.
Underground: South Kensington
www.nhm.ac.uk

THE NATURAL HISTORY MUSEUM

THE BIRTHPLACE OF BRITISH MOTORSPORT AND AVIATION

THE Spirit OF BROOKLANDS

- The Museum covers 30 acres of the original site.
- Exhibits feature a fine collection of historic racing cars, aircraft and bicycles.
- Bertie Bear Trail and family activities.
- Tailored school programmes.
- Walk through aircraft exhibits.
- All event days are open to the public.
- Free parking and trail guide.
- Tea Rooms open all day.

Adults £7, Students & Senior Citizens £6, Children 6-16 £5, 5 and under FREE. Family ticket £18. Open: Tuesday-Sunday 10-5 summer 10-4 winter.

Brooklands Museum, Brooklands Road, Weybridge, Surrey KT13 0QN Tel: 01932 857381
Email: brooklands@dial.pipex.com
Internet: www.motor-software.co.uk/brooklands

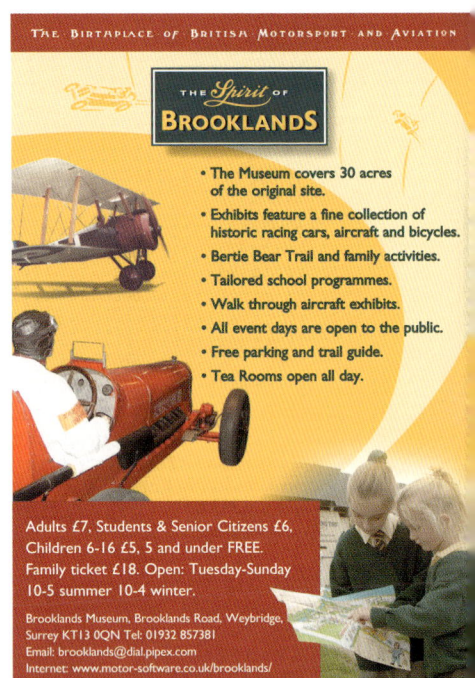

London's newest and most exciting attraction

A GREAT NEW SPORTS DAY OUT
FOR ALL THE FAMILY

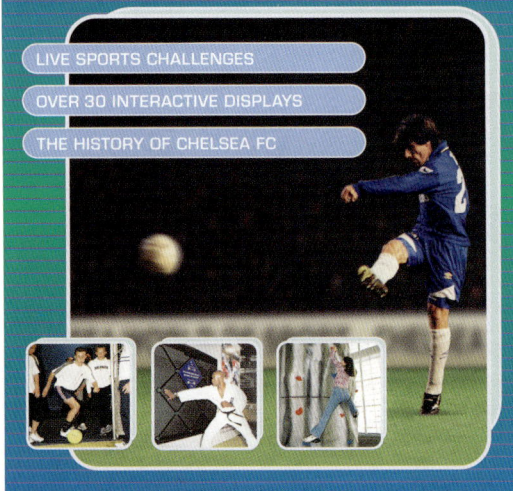

- LIVE SPORTS CHALLENGES
- OVER 30 INTERACTIVE DISPLAYS
- THE HISTORY OF CHELSEA FC

Take on the best and win at Chelsea World of Sport in our live sporting challenges. Test your ball control skills and shooting ability. Can you beat the throw-in world record? Put your tennis shots to the test. How fast are you out of the blocks? How quick are your reactions? There's a challenge for everyone at Chelsea World of Sport. Call us now on 020 7915 2222 and book your place in sporting history.

CHELSEA WORLD OF SPORT AT CHELSEA VILLAGE

FOR INFORMATION CALL: 020 7915 2222
or visit: www.chelseaworldofsport.com

Fulham Road, London ⊖ Fulham Broadway

....CHELSEA WORLD OF SPORT....WHERE SCIENCE MEETS SPORT...

Fun Learning & Activity Holidays for 8 - 17 year olds

CLAC

Residential or Non-Residential Courses
at Lavant House or Slindon College, Sussex

Weekly during July and August

French, German, Spanish

or English as a foreign language

accredited by
The British Council

★ Lively International Atmosphere
★ Make friends from many different countries
★ Practise and improve a language naturally
★ On-campus swimming pool, squash, playing fields,
  Horse-riding, art, drama, cookery, parties, discos etc.
★ Excursions, shopping and sightseeing trips.

Cambridge Language & Activity Courses
10 Shelford Park Avenue, Great Shelford, Cambridge CB2 5LU
Tel: 01223 846348 / 562360   Email: anne@clac.org.uk
www.clac.org.uk

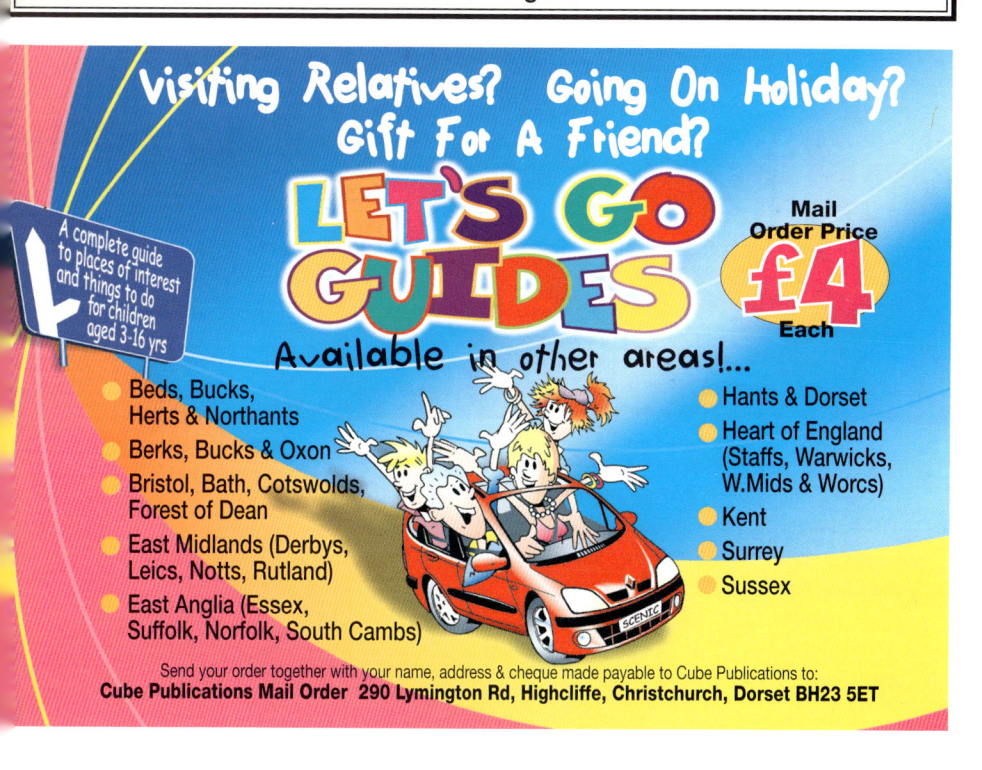

Visiting Relatives? Going On Holiday? Gift For A Friend?

LET'S GO GUIDES

A complete guide to places of interest and things to do for children aged 3-16 yrs

Mail Order Price £4 Each

Available in other areas!...

- Beds, Bucks, Herts & Northants
- Berks, Bucks & Oxon
- Bristol, Bath, Cotswolds, Forest of Dean
- East Midlands (Derbys, Leics, Notts, Rutland)
- East Anglia (Essex, Suffolk, Norfolk, South Cambs)
- Hants & Dorset
- Heart of England (Staffs, Warwicks, W.Mids & Worcs)
- Kent
- Surrey
- Sussex

Send your order together with your name, address & cheque made payable to Cube Publications to:
Cube Publications Mail Order 290 Lymington Rd, Highcliffe, Christchurch, Dorset BH23 5ET

Explore Oceans Time and Space for Free

Encounter Nelson's bloodstained uniform from Trafalgar. Take the helm of a Viking longboat, or fire a cannon. Span East and West astride the Meridian Line. See the original Harrison clocks or gaze at the stars in the home of Greenwich Mean Time. Entry is now free, though there may be charges for some special events and exhibitions. Beyond, there's even more to see – the Cutty Sark, the Old Royal Naval College and the Royal Park.
Open 10:00 – 17:00. Call 020 8312 6565 or visit www.nmm.ac.uk

NATIONAL MARITIME MUSEUM   **ROYAL OBSERVATORY GREENWICH**

Maritime GREENWICH WORLD HERITAGE SITE   Travel: Rail or riverboat to Greenwich. Docklands Light Railway to Cutty Sark. From M25 via A2 or M11/A12.

CRÉATEUR D' AUTOMOBILES | **RENAULT**

Safety for all
RENAULT

A Renault Commitment

Safety is a key priority for Renault so it is not surprising that, across the range, Renault cars scored top marks in the EuroNCAP safety tests. But Renault's commitment to safety does not stop at safe cars. As part of Renault's pan European campaign to educate primary children to stay safe on the roads, Renault UK has provided 'Safety Matters' road safety teaching kits to Primary schools throughout the UK.

For more information write to: Safety Matters, ANG 8097, Diss, Norfolk IP98 3HH.

Top Marks for Safety

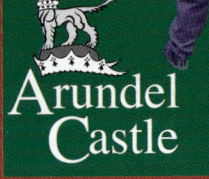

Historic Sites, Castles, Museums & Science Centres

Step back in time and find out about days gone by, or step into the future and imagine yourself in the next century. Art, history, science and technology find a place here.

A1

(B) **Bircham Windmill,** Great Bircham. This restored 19th Century working windmill
Schools and bakery transports you back to a bygone era of rural Norfolk. Relax in the tea rooms, while the children mix with the ponies and small animals. Cycle hire available. Open daily, Easter-30th Sept, 10am-5pm. 01485 578393.

(B) **Castle Rising Castle,** NE of King's Lynn, is an imposing 12th century castle. The
Schools keep and ramparts still survive and a taped tour guide enlivens this splendid example of a
Open all year Norman Castle. Open daily, 1st Apr-1st Nov, 10am-6pm; Wed-Sun, 2nd Nov-31st Mar, 10am-4pm; closed 25th/26th Dec. 01553 631330.

(A) **Lynn Museum,** Market Street, King's Lynn. Explore town life through the ages as
Schools King's Lynn grew and thrived. Phone for details of a changing programme of events and
Open all year activities. Open Tues-Sat, 10am-5pm. 01553 775001. www.west-norfolk.gov.uk

(D) **Sandringham,** NE of King's Lynn, the country retreat of HM the Queen, includes 600 acres of grounds and lakes. There is a museum and visitor centre, while the country park offers tractor and trailer tours. Open daily, 30th Mar-23rd Jul (closed 18th Jul) and 7th Aug-27th Oct, 11am-4.45pm. 01553 772675.

(B) **The Old Gaol House,** Saturday Market Place, King's Lynn. A personal audio tour
Schools guide leads you through the old 1930s police station and 18th and 19th century prison
Open all year cells. Children can create their own fingerprint tests and have a mugshot taken. Open daily, Easter-Oct, 10am-5pm (last admission 4.15pm); Fri-Tues, Nov-Easter. Closed 25th, 26th Dec. 01553 774297. www.west-norfolk.gov.uk

(B) **Town House Museum of Lynn Life,** 46 Queen St, King's Lynn. The past of
Schools this once-thriving port is brought to life through exhibits, ranging from costumes and
Open all year toys, to historic room displays, including a working Victorian kitchen and 1950s living room. Open May-Sept, Mon-Sat, 10am-5pm, Sun, 2-5pm; Oct-Apr, Mon-Sat, 10am-4pm; closed 25th, 26th Dec and Bank Hols. 01553 773450.

(B) **True's Yard,** 3-5 North St, King's Lynn. These two tiny cottages, now transformed
Schools into a museum, offer a children's corner, research facilities, craft demonstrations, tea
Open all year rooms and a gift shop. Open daily Apr-Sept, 9.30am-4.30pm (last admissions 3.45pm); Nov-Mar, Mon-Sat; closed Christmas-New Year. 01553 770479.

A2

(B) **Collectors World** and **The Magical Dickens Experience,** Hermitage Hall,
Schools Downham Market, on A1122 beside Downham Bridge. An eccentric and extensive mixture,
Open all year from cars to cameras, the Swinging Sixties to Norfolk hero Nelson - and lots more besides. Plus a Pets Corner and river and farm walks. Open daily, 11am-5pm (last entrance 4pm). Groups by appointment. 01366 383185. www.collectors-world.com

(B) **Denver Windmill,** Denver, close to A10, SW of Downham Market, is a fully restored
Schools working windmill. Guided tours and a climb up the windmill give wonderful views. There is
Open all year a visitor centre, craft workshops, bakery and tea shop. Special educational visits organised, where pupils can make their own bread. Open daily, Apr-Sept, 10am-5pm, Oct-Mar, 10am-4pm; closed 24th-26th Dec. 01366 384009.

(C) **Oxburgh Hall,** NT, Oxborough, is a 15th century, red-brick manor house, surrounded
Schools by a magnificent water-filled moat. Trails for children and a special guide book (small charge) point out things of interest, including the Catholic priest's hole. Delightful woodland walks. Open 23rd Mar-3rd Nov, Sat-Wed, 1-5pm (last admission 4.30pm); 11am-5pm on Bank Hol Mons. Gardens open 2nd-17th Mar, Sat and Sun, 11am-4pm, 23rd Mar-3rd Nov, Sat-Wed, 11am-5.30pm, and daily in Aug. 01366 328258. www.nationaltrust.org.uk

---

Price Codes for a family of four: (A): less than £5 (B): £5-£10 (C): £10-£15 (D): £15-£20 (E): £20-£30 (G): £30-£50 (H): Over £50 (F): Free
Map Ref: Grid square on Page 2 Map   Schools: Facilities available   ● Birthday parties

MAP REFS **PRICE CODES**

A3

Ⓓ Schools **Anglesey Abbey,** NT, sign posted off A14, E of **Cambridge**, has an outstanding 100 acre garden. The house contains a collection of paintings, furniture and clocks. The Lode watermill grinds corn the 1st Saturday of each month. A children's guide to the house is available. 01223 811200. www.nationaltrust.org.uk/angleseyabbey

Ⓓ Schools **Audley End House and Park,** EH, near **Saffron Walden**, on the B1383. A gorgeous Jacobean palace revealing a wealth of architecture and furniture. Open 29th Mar-2nd Oct, Wed-Sun and Bank Hol Mons, 1-5pm. Park and gardens 11am-5pm. 2nd-31st Oct, 11am-4pm. Park and gardens, 11am-5pm. Last admission 1 hour earlier. 01799 522399. Education Service, 01223 582700. www.english-heritage.org.uk

Ⓐ Schools Open all year **Braintree Museum,** Manor Street, **Braintree**, displays the development of the area from the earliest times to the present day, including the important local textile industry. Open Mon-Sat and Bank Hol Mons 10am-5pm. 01376 325266. www.braintree.gov.uk

Ⓑ Schools Open all year **Cambridge and County Folk Museum,** Castle Street, **Cambridge**. This popular museum is quite small but has wide ranging displays of artefacts illustrating everyday life from the 17th century to the present day. Workshops and activity days for children. Pushchair access limited. Open Apr-Sept, Mon-Sat, 10.30am-5pm, Sun, 2-5pm; Closed Mons, Oct-Mar. Closed Christmas and Good Fri. 01223 355159. www.folkmuseum.org.uk

Ⓕ Schools Open all year **Cambridge Darkroom,** Gwydir Street. See "Free Places" chapter.

Ⓑ Schools **Cambridge Museum of Technology,** Cheddars Lane, is run by volunteers and housed in a preserved Victorian pumping station - just look for the chimney! Open every Sun 2-5pm, Easter-Oct. 1st Sun of the month, Nov-Easter plus special steam and model railway weekends 11am-5pm. 01223 368650.

Ⓕ Schools Open all year **Cambridge University Collection of Air Photographs,** Free School Lane. See Whipple Museum in "Free Places" chapter.

Ⓕ Schools Open all year **Fitzwilliam Museum,** Trumpington Street, **Cambridge**. See "Free Places" chapter.

Ⓒ Schools Open all year **House on the Hill Museum Adventure,** Stansted Mountfitchet, adjacent to the Castle, incorporates the largest toy museum in Europe, as well as a rock 'n' roll film and theatre experience, and an "end of the pier" amusement machine fun zone. Open daily, 10am-5pm, 4pm in Winter. Closed 24th-26th Dec. 01279 813767. www.gold.enta.net

Ⓓ Schools Open all year **Imperial War Museum,** Duxford, on the M11, S of Cambridge. Many famous aircraft, some of which fly on Summer Sundays. There is an artillery and a new Far Eastern exhibition. Adventure playground and picnic area. Under 16s free. Pleasure flights available Summer weekends (for details phone 0870 9026146). Open daily, 10am-6pm, 4pm in Winter. Closed 24th-26th Dec. 01223 835000. www.iwm.org.uk

Ⓕ Schools Open all year **Kettles Yard,** Castle Street, **Cambridge**. See "Free Places" chapter.

Ⓓ Schools **Mountfitchet Castle and Norman Village,** Stansted Mountfitchet, is an 11th century Motte and Bailey castle and village reconstructed on its original, ancient site. You can see, through domestic buildings, models and livestock, how life was in the medieval period. Open daily, 2nd Sun Mar-2nd Sun Nov, 10am-5pm. 01279 813237. www.gold.enta.net

Ⓑ Schools 🎈 **National Horseracing Museum,** 99 High Street, **Newmarket**. This award-winning museum has two special exhibitions "The World of Dick Francis" and "Royalty and Racing - a Jubilee Exhibition". The Practical Gallery and "hands-on" displays remain unchanged and tours of racing establishments are available. Open 2nd Apr-end Oct, Tues-Sun 10am-5pm, also Mons in Jul and Aug, and all Bank Hols. 01638 667333. www.nhrm.co.uk

---

Price Codes for a family of four: Ⓐ: less than £5 Ⓑ: £5-£10 Ⓒ: £10-£15 Ⓓ: £15-£20 Ⓔ: £20-£30 Ⓖ: £30-£50 Ⓗ: Over £50 Ⓕ: Free
Map Ref: Grid square on Page 2 Map   Schools: Facilities available   🎈 Birthday parties

Historic Sites, Castles, Museums & Science Centres

A3 Ⓐ Schools Open all year **Saffron Walden Museum,** Museum Street. Permanent displays on the "Ages of Man", "Worlds of Man" and Ancient Egypt are supplemented with changing displays. Pride of place goes to Wallace the Lion! Award-winning Natural History Discovery Centre. Open daily, except 24th & 25th Dec, Mar-Oct, Mon-Sat, 10am-5pm; Suns & Bank Hols, 2-5pm. Nov-Feb, Mon-Sat, 10am-4.30pm; Suns & Bank Hols, 2-4.30pm. 01799 510333.

Ⓕ Schools Open all year **Sedgwick Museum of Geology,** Downing Street, Cambridge. See "Free Places" chapter.

Ⓕ Schools Open all year **University Museum of Archaeology and Anthropology,** Downing Street, Cambridge. See "Free Places" chapter.

Ⓕ Schools Open all year **University Museum of Zoology,** Downing Street, Cambridge. See "Free Places" chapter.

Ⓕ Schools Open all year **Whipple Museum of History of Science,** Free School Lane, Cambridge. See "Free Places" chapter.

Ⓓ Schools **Wimpole Hall,** NT, off the A603, SW of Cambridge, is an 18th century mansion, set in 300 acres of parkland. A children's guide to the house is available and there is a farm display in the Great Barn. (See also "Farms" chapter for adjacent Home Farm. Joint ticket available for Hall and Farm.) Open 23rd Mar-3rd Nov, Tues-Thurs (Fri in Aug), Sat & Sun, 1-5pm; Bank Hols, 11am-5pm. 01223 207257. www.wimpole.org

A4 Ⓕ Open all year **Abbey Church,** Waltham Abbey. See "Free Places" chapter.

Ⓑ Schools 🍭 **Barleylands Farm and Museum,** Barleylands Road, just off A129 near Billericay, has exhibits including tractors, steam engines and farm implements together with farm animals and a children's play area. It also houses glass-blowing, a blacksmith and craft shops. A narrow gauge steam railway operates on Suns and Bank Hols in Summer, weather permitting. Open Mar-Oct, daily 10am-5pm. Closed Sats in Aug. 01268 290229. (See "Farms" chapter.)

Ⓕ Schools Open all year **Chelmsford Museum,** Oaklands Park, Moulsham Street. See "Free Places" chapter.

Ⓕ Schools Open all year **Epping Forest District Museum,** Sun Street, Waltham Abbey. See "Free Places" chapter.

Ⓕ Schools Open all year **Lee Valley Information Centre,** Abbey Gardens at Waltham Abbey. See "Free Places" chapter.

Ⓕ **National Motorboat Museum,** Pitsea. See "Free Places" chapter.

Ⓒ Schools Open all year **Secret Nuclear Bunker,** Kelvedon Hatch, on the A128 to Brentwood. A unique and intriguing experience. Step inside the door of a deceptive rural bungalow and discover the labyrinthine, twilight world of the Cold War. Canteen for refreshments. Open daily, Mar-Oct, 10am-4pm (5pm Sat, Sun & Bank Hols). Nov-Feb, Thurs-Sun, 10am-4pm. 01277 364883. www.japar.demon.co.uk

Ⓕ Open all year **Thurrock Local History Museum,** Grays. See "Free Places" chapter.

Ⓑ Schools Open all year **Tilbury Fort.** EH. The massive star-shaped fortifications encompass an enormous parade ground equipped with cannon. There is an underground passageway once used to store ammunition and a military museum. There's even a chance to fire an anti-aircraft gun. Free children's activity sheet. Open daily, 10am-6pm or dusk, Apr-Sept; Wed-Sun, 10am-4pm, Nov-Mar. Closed Christmas. 01375 858489, Education Service, 01223 582715.

B1 Ⓓ Schools **Blickling Hall,** NT, Blickling. This fine 17th century Jacobean house has a walled garden, orangery, lake and walks, with picnic area and shop. Children are welcomed with a special guide and menu, scribble sheets, play area and garden quizzes. See also Blickling Park in "Free Places" chapter. Open 23rd Mar-3rd Nov, Wed-Sun 1-4.30pm. 01263 738030. www.nationaltrust.org.uk

---

Price Codes for a family of four: Ⓐ: less than £5 Ⓑ: £5-£10 Ⓒ: £10-£15 Ⓓ: £15-£20 Ⓔ: £20-£30 Ⓖ: £30-£50 Ⓗ: Over £50 Ⓕ: Free
Map Ref: Grid square on Page 2 Map   Schools: Facilities available   🍭 Birthday parties

MAP REFS	PRICE CODES		
B1	Ⓕ Schools	**Cromer Lifeboat & Museum,** The Pier and Gangway, **Cromer**. See "Free Places" chapter.	
	Ⓑ Schools Open all year	**Cromer Museum,** East Cottages, Tucker Street, **Cromer**. A late-Victorian fisherman's cottage is the scene for a wealth of local seaside and fishing history and memorabilia. Regular events and talks throughout the year help bring the past to life. Open daily, Mon-Sat, 10am-5pm (closed Mon, 1-2pm), Sun 2-5pm; closed 25th/26th Dec and 1st Jan. 01263 513543. www.norfolk.gov.uk/tourism/museums	
	Ⓒ Schools	**Felbrigg Hall,** NT, **Felbrigg**. A fine 17th century house with wonderful park and woodland, with some walks suitable for pushchairs. A scavenger hunt keeps primary age children amused outside, while a children's guidebook (small charge) points out things of interest in the house. Grounds open daily all year, dawn to dusk. Hall and gardens open Apr-Oct, Sat-Wed and Bank Hols, 11am-4.30pm. 01263 83744. www.nationaltrust.org.uk	
	Ⓔ	**Holkham Hall,** Wells-next-the-Sea. Palladian-style stately home with large bygones museum. Enjoy a boat cruise on the lake or visit the nursery, gardens, pottery and restaurant. The History of Farming Museum is aimed particularly at children. Holkham beach is nearby. (Small parking fee charged). Open 26th May-30th Sept, Sun-Thurs 1-5pm; Easter, May, Spring and Summer Bank Hols, 11.30am-5pm. 01328 710227. www.holkham.co.uk	
	Ⓒ	**Houghton Hall,** Houghton, was built in the early 18th century for Sir Robert Walpole. Wander through the 350 acres of rolling parkland and see the extensive collection of 20,000 model soldiers and militaria. Also of interest are the walled garden, picnic area and gift shop. Open Thurs and Sun, Easter Sun-last Sun in Sept, 1-5.30pm (house opens at 2pm; last admissions 5pm). 01485 528569. wwws.houghtonhall.com	
	Ⓑ Schools Open all year	**Langham Glass,** The Long Barn, North Street, **Langham**, gives a rare opportunity to view the master glass-maker in action. The restored 18th century barn complex houses a glass-blowing workshop, museum, factory shop and adventure playground for children. Open daily Easter-31st Oct, 10am-5pm; Nov-Apr, glass making, Mon-Fri; no admission charge during Winter months. 01328 830511. www.langhamglass.co.uk	
	Ⓑ Schools Open all year	**Letheringsett Watermill,** Riverside Road, **Letheringsett**. Built in 1802, this fully restored, water-powered flour mill with resident ducks demonstrates the old traditions of making flour. Open 28th May-Oct, Mon-Fri, 10am-5pm, Sat 9am-1pm; Nov-27th May Tues-Thurs, 9am-4pm. Working demonstrations, Tues-Fri, 2-4.30pm; closed Christmas. 01263 713153. www.letheringsettwatermill.co.uk	
	Ⓒ	**Muckleburgh Collection,** Weybourne. Original World War II buildings house a collection of over 136 military vehicles, used by the allied armies during and since the Second World War. Also on display are over 600 models of military vehicles and aircraft. Special tank demonstration days every Sun, daily during school holidays. Open daily, 17th Feb-27th Oct, 10am-5pm. 01263 588210. www.muckleburgh.co.uk	
	Ⓐ Schools	**Shell Museum,** Glandford, near **Blakeney**. Built in 1915 by Sir Alfred Jodrell to house his beautiful and unique collection of sea shells, jewels, fossils and minerals. Open Easter Sat-31st Oct, 10am-12.30pm and 2-4.30pm; closed Sun and Mon. 01263 740081.	
	Ⓐ Schools	**Sheringham Museum,** Station Road. Exhibits weave the story of life in the town to include fishing and boat building, the war years, tourism, the beach, lacemaking and lifeboats. Souvenirs and mementoes are available from the shop. Open Tues-Sat, Easter-31st Oct, 10am-4pm, Sun, 2-4pm. 01263 821871. www.sheringhammuseum.co.uk	
	Ⓑ Schools	**The Shirehall (Courthouse) Museum,** Walsingham. Put yourself in the dock in the Georgian courtroom - or be the judge. Also pay a visit to the cells and the site of the prisoners' treadmill. Open Easter-end Oct, daily, 10am-4.30pm. 01328 820510.	

Price Codes for a family of four: Ⓐ: less than £5   Ⓑ: £5-£10   Ⓒ: £10-£15   Ⓓ: £15-£20   Ⓔ: £20-£30   Ⓖ: £30-£50   Ⓗ: Over £50   Ⓕ: Free
Map Ref: Grid square on Page 2 Map   Schools: Facilities available   ● Birthday parties

Historic Sites, Castles, Museums & Science Centres

MAP REFS | **PRICE CODES**

B1 © Schools **Thursford Collection,** Thursford Green. This spectacular collection of giant mechanical organs includes a Wurlitzer, with daily live musical shows. Enjoy the thrill of the Venetian Gondola Switchback rides. There is a children's play area and picnic area. Open daily, Good Fri-20th Oct, 12-5pm. Christmas shows during Nov and Dec. 01328 878477.

Ⓐ Schools **Wells Maritime Museum,** Wells Harbour Office, Wells-next-the-Sea. Small museum of maritime memorabilia with displays covering fishing, the port, the coastguard and the lifeboat. Open Good Fri-Oct half term, Tues-Fri, 2-5pm; Sat, Sun, Bank Hol Mon, 11am-5pm.

B2 Ⓕ Schools **100th Bomb Group Memorial Museum,** Common Road, Dickleburgh. See "Free Places" chapter.

Ⓐ / Ⓕ Schools Open all year **Ancient House Museum,** White Hart Street, Thetford. A 15th century timber-framed merchant's house, now a museum, reveals Thetford's link with an Indian prince and Breckland's natural history. Free admission Sept-Jun. Open all year Mon-Sat, 10am-5pm (closed 12.30-1pm), Jun-Aug, Sun, 2-5pm; closed 25th, 26th Dec, 1st Jan. 01842 752599. www.paston.co.uk/users/ncm/nms_home.html

Ⓕ **Bishop Bonner's Cottages Museum,** Dereham. See "Free Places" chapter.

Ⓔ Schools 🍭 **Bressingham Steam Experience & Gardens,** near Diss, has delights for both adults and children, with over 5 miles of narrow gauge steam rides through woodland (extra charge per person) and over 50 steam engines to see. Special events include the chance to drive your own steam engine. Open daily, Easter-end Oct, 10.30am-5.30pm (4.30pm Mar and Oct.) National Dad's Army Exhibition open all year. 01379 687382. www.bressingham.co.uk

Ⓑ Schools **Bridewell Museum,** Bridewell Alley, Norwich. Discover the historic secrets of local industries, from mustard and shoes to textiles and beer. Exhibits include reconstructions of a 1920s pharmacy and a 1930s pawnbroker's shop. Fun activities are organised during school holidays. Open Feb-end Oct, Mon-Sat, 10am-5pm. 01603 667228.

Ⓕ Schools Open all year **Burston Strike School,** The Village Green, Burston. See "Free Places" chapter.

Ⓕ Open all year **Caister St Edmund,** near Norwich. See "Free Places" chapter.

Ⓑ / Ⓕ Schools Open all year **Castle Acre Priory & Castle,** EH. On the edge of this pretty village lie the ruins of a double-moated Norman castle, with impressive earthworks (free entry). Also the ruins of Britain's best preserved Cluniac Priory. An audio tour is available. Open daily Apr-Oct, 10am-6pm, Nov-28th Mar, Wed-Sun, 10am-4pm, closed 1-2pm; closed 24th, 25th, 26th Dec and 1st Jan. 01760 755394. Schools, 01223 582732. www.english-heritage.org.uk

Ⓑ Schools Open all year **City of Norwich Aviation Museum,** Old Norwich Road, Horsham St. Faith. A collection of aircraft and memorabilia tell the aviation history of Norfolk, and includes the 100 Group Memorial Museum. Open Apr-Oct, Tues-Sat, 10am-5pm, Sun 12-5pm; Nov-Mar, Wed and Sat, 10am-4pm, Sun 12-4pm; closed Christmas to New Year. 01603 893080. www.cnam.co.uk

Ⓑ Schools Open all year **Dragon Hall,** 115-123 King Street, Norwich. A magnificent medieval merchant's hall, with a timber-frame structure. It takes its name from the intricately carved and painted dragon in the crown post roof. Open Apr-Oct, Mon-Sat, 10am-4pm; Nov-Mar, Mon-Fri, 10am-4pm; closed Bank Hols and Christmas to New Year. 01603 663922. http://freespace.virgin.net/dragon.hall/index.htm

© Schools Open all year 🍭 **EcoTech,** Turbine Way, Swaffham, is an environmental discovery centre with interactive displays and touch-screen computers. Climb the UK's largest wind turbine (small additional fee). Special education packs are available and the Rainforest café has a soft play area for younger children. There is also a picnic area and gift shop. Open 1st Mar-31st Oct, daily 10am-5pm; 1st Nov-28th Feb, Mon-Fri, 10am-4pm; closed 24th-26th Dec and 1st Jan. 01760 726100. www.ecotech.org.uk

---

Price Codes for a family of four: Ⓐ: less than £5 Ⓑ: £5-£10 ©: £10-£15 Ⓓ: £15-£20 Ⓔ: £20-£30 Ⓖ: £30-£50 Ⓗ: Over £50 Ⓕ: Free
Map Ref: Grid square on Page 2 Map   Schools: Facilities available   🍭 Birthday parties

MAP REFS	PRICE CODES
B2	

Forncett Industrial Steam Museum, Low Road, **Forncett St Mary.** Britain's industrial past lives again as these huge machines - including the engine once used to raise London's Tower Bridge - are coaxed into hissing motion. Open May-Nov, 1st Sun in every month, 11am-5pm (schools by appointment). 01508 488277. www.oldenginehouse.demon.co.uk/Forncett.htm
(B) Schools

Grimes Graves, EH, **Lynford,** 7 miles NW of Thetford, off A134. These 4,000-year old Neolithic flint mines give a glimpse into the world of stone-age man. Free children's activity sheet. Participate in the flint knapping demonstration days and 'meet' stone-age man! Open daily Apr-Oct, 10am-6pm or dusk (closed 1-2pm); Wed-Sun, 1st Nov-28th Mar, 10am-4pm (last admissions half an hour before closing); closed 24th-26th Dec and 1st Jan. 01842 810656. Schools, 01223 582500. www.english-heritage.org.uk
(B) Schools Open all year

Iceni Village and Museums, Cockley Cley. On what is believed to be the original site, this reconstruction of an Iceni tribal village offers spacious fields for children to run free, a nature trail and bird hide. The barn complex houses agricultural machinery and a World War II room. A medieval cottage still stands on the site and there is a forge with museums. Open daily Apr-Oct, 11am-5.30pm (10am, Jul and Aug). 01760 724588.
(C) Schools

Inspire Hands-On Science Centre, St Michaels Church, Coslany Street, Norwich. Set in a restored medieval church, this futuristic science centre encourages all ages to explore the wonders and curiosities of the world of science. Science shop, light refreshments and special shows. Open daily, 10am-5.30pm. 01603 612612. www.science-project.org
(C) Schools Open all year

The Mustard Shop, 15 Royal Arcade, **Norwich.** Shopping spiced with history, the story of Jeremiah Colman - and a mustard trail for children to discover his adventures. Open Mon-Sat, 9.30am-5pm, Bank Hols, 10am-4pm. 01603 627889.
(F) Open all year

Norwich Castle Museum, Castle Meadow, **Norwich.** Newly refurbished, you can explore the castle's Norman keep, discover East Anglian Queen Boudica's struggle with the Romans and see relics of her tribes' gold treasures. There are many hands-on exhibits, a fine art collection, excellent research facilities, a lecture theatre, shop and café. Opening times and admission charges, call 01603 493625.
Schools Open all year

Origins - The History Mix, The Forum, Millennium Plain, Theatre St, **Norwich.** Interact and learn about the city of Norwich - its past, and its place in the region. A wealth of information is presented in an imaginative and stimulating way. For opening times call the 24 hour Info Line: 01603 727920. www.theforumnorwich.com
(C) Schools Open all year

Roots of Norfolk at Gressenhall - Norfolk Rural Life Museum, Gressenhall. Experience life as it was in the past for the ordinary people of Norfolk - the village street and its shops, the workhouse, the countryside. Quizzes, colouring sheets and Explorer Packs for children, costumed characters, story telling and craft demonstrations, plus an adventure playground - a lot on offer to bring history back to life. Open daily, 24th Mar-3rd Nov, 10am-5pm. 01362 860563. (See also "Farms" chapter.) www.norfolk.gov.uk/tourism/museums
(C) Schools

Royal Norfolk Regimental Museum, Shirehall, Market Avenue, **Norwich.** This museum tells the story of the county regiment in peace and war since 1685. Videos, exhibits, photographs and memorabilia plus a reconstructed World War I trench with sound effects. Open 10am-5pm, Mon-Sat, 2-5pm, Sun; closed Good Fri, 25th, 26th Dec and 1st Jan. 01603 223649. www.norfolk.gov.uk/tourism/museums
(B) Schools Open all year

Sainsbury Centre for Visual Arts, University of East Anglia, Earlham Road, Norwich. This collection is housed in an award-winning building, on the site of the University of East Anglia. On the first Sun of each month, there is live music and a table of activities aimed at children. Open Tues-Sun, 11am-5pm; closed 23rd Dec-2nd Jan. 01603 592468. Schools, 01603 593199. www.vea.ak.uk/scva
(B) Schools Open all year

Price Codes for a family of four: **A**: less than £5 **B**: £5-£10 **C**: £10-£15 **D**: £15-£20 **E**: £20-£30 **G**: £30-£50 **H**: Over £50 **F**: Free
Map Ref: Grid square on Page 2 Map   Schools: Facilities available   ● Birthday parties

Historic Sites, Castles, Museums & Science Centres

MAP REFS	PRICE CODES	
B2	ⒷOpen all year	**Strangers' Hall**, Charing Cross, **Norwich**. This is one of the city's oldest and finest buildings, typical of the merchants' houses when Norwich was in its heyday. Visits by guided tour only, Easter-Sept, 11am, 1pm and 3pm; Oct-Easter, Wed and Sat, 11am and 1pm. Tours restricted to 15 people, book in advance from **Castle Museum**. 01603 493625.
	ⒶSchools	**Swaffham Museum**, Town Hall, 4 London Street, **Swaffham**. Set in the former home of the town's brewer, this is a small social history museum. Special education and research facilities. Open Apr-Oct, Tues-Sat, 11am-4pm, Sun, 12-4pm. (Open all year for schools.) 01760 721230. www.aboutswaffham.co.uk
	ⒷSchools Open all year	**Wingfield College and Gardens**, on the B1118, near **Stradbroke**, comprises an historic 14th century house, topiary gardens and duck pond. Interior highlights include the old kitchens and the oak-timbered Great Hall. Exhibitions in the College Yard Visitors' Centre. Open Easter-end Sept, weekends and Bank Hol Mons, 2-6pm. 01379 384888.
	ⒶSchools	**Wymondham Heritage Museum**, The Bridewell, Norwich Road, **Wymondham**. This award-winning museum, has many displays of local interest. Special activities, an audio-visual presentation and a visit to the cells make this an interesting visit for children. Open Mar-Nov, 10am-4pm, Mon-Sat, 2-4pm, Sun. 01953 600205. Schools and groups, 01362 850154.
B3	Tour Ⓐ	**Abbey Visitors' Centre at Samson's Tower**, Abbey Gardens , **Bury St. Edmunds**, (see also "Free Places" chapter). The Abbey ruins are brought to life through hands-on activities, an audio tour and high-tech displays in the centre. Open daily, 10am-5pm, Apr-Oct. 01284 763110.
	ⒸSchools Open all year	**Anglo-Saxon Village**, West Stow, **Bury St. Edmunds**. An early Anglo-Saxon village reconstructed where excavated. Fascinating introduction video available. Anglo-Saxon Centre opened in 1999 with original objects found on the site. Free parking, adventure play area, shop and café. Open daily, 10am-5pm (last admission 4pm). Closed Christmas. 01284 728718. www.stedmundsbury.gov.uk/weststow.htm
	Ⓑ	**Bourne Mill**, NT, off the B1025, S of **Colchester**. A water mill, originally a 16th century fishing lodge. Open Bank Hol Suns and Mons, Suns and Tues Jun-Aug, 2-5pm. 01206 572422. www.nationaltrust.org.uk
	ⒻSchools Open all year	**Christchurch Mansion and Wolsey Art Gallery**, Ipswich. See "Free Places" chapter.
	ⒶSchools	**Coggeshall Grange Barn**, NT, off A120, is the earliest surviving timber-framed barn in Europe, dating back to 1140. Its size is impressive and it has an interesting history well worth discovering. Open 2nd Apr-15th Oct, Tues, Thurs, Sun and Bank Hol Mons, 2-5pm. 01376 562226. www.nationaltrust.org.uk
	ⒸSchools Open all year	**Colchester Castle**, houses an excellent museum reflecting the town's rich history from prehistoric times to the Civil War. Lots of "hands-on" displays and, for the brave, an audio-visual drama of the story of the castle prisons. Open Mon-Sat, 10am-5pm & Suns, 11am-5pm. 01206 282939. Education Officer: 01206 282918. www.colchestermuseum.org.uk
	ⒹSchools	**Colne Valley Railway**, Castle Hedingham, on the A1017, recreates a busy rural railway station of yesteryear. Enjoy taking a ride in one of the most pleasant parts of the Colne Valley. There is a programme of "Steam Days" and special events throughout the year when rides are available. Phone for free time-table of open times and events. Also access to Colne Valley Farm Park. Farm open May-Sept 10am-4pm. 01787 461174. www.cvr.org.uk
	ⒻOpen all year	**Dedham Art & Craft Centre and Toy Museum**, High St, **Dedham**. See "Free Places" chapter.

Price Codes for a family of four: Ⓐ: less than £5   Ⓑ: £5-£10   Ⓒ: £10-£15   Ⓓ: £15-£20   Ⓔ: £20-£30   Ⓖ: £30-£50   Ⓗ: Over £50   Ⓕ: Free
Map Ref: Grid square on Page 2 Map   Schools: Facilities available   ● Birthday parties

MAP REFS	PRICE CODES
B3	

Ⓑ / ⓒ **East Anglian Railway Museum,** just off the A1124 at **Chappel** is a busily
Schools expanding working museum. There are collections of vintage carriages and steam engines
Open all year of all types. On special Operating Days you can enjoy a nostalgic train ride. Open daily,
10am-5pm. Closed Christmas. Regular "Operating Days", Mar-Dec. 01206 242524.
www.earm.co.uk

ⓒ / Ⓓ **Essex Secret Bunker,** Mistley, near **Manningtree** on the B1352. Built in 1951 and
Schools operational until 1993, the bunker was the County nuclear war HQ for Essex. Cinemas/
Open all year sound effects and displays bring the bunker to life, as you explore the secret passages,
offices and operations areas used during the cold war. Open daily, Mar-Oct, 10.30am-5pm
(6pm Aug). Nov-Feb, Sat & Sun only, 10.30am-4.30pm. Closed 20th Dec-5th Jan. 01206
392271. www.essexsecretbunker.com

Ⓑ **Gainsborough's House,** Gainsborough Street, **Sudbury.** Birthplace of Thomas
Schools Gainsborough, housing a good collection of the artist's work. Open daily (except Good Fri,
Open all year Christmas and New Year), 31st Mar-end Oct, Tues-Sat 10am-5pm, Sun 2-5pm, Nov-Easter,
Tues-Sat, 10am-4pm, Sun, 2-4pm. Open Bank Hol Mons. 01787 372958.
www.gainsborough.org

Ⓑ **Gosfield Hall,** Gosfield, near Halstead. This Tudor courtyard house with Georgian
additions has been partially converted into apartments for retired people, but the main
rooms are open to the public. Afternoon teas and plant sales. Open May-Sept, Wed &
Thurs 2-5pm. Guided tours at 2.30 and 3.15pm. 01787 472914.

Ⓐ **Harwich Lifeboat Museum,** The Old Lifeboat Station, small but interesting,
Schools houses the last Clacton, "34ft" off-shore lifeboat. Climb aboard and stand at the helm.
Displays and a video of daring and hair-raising rescues will keep the children fascinated.
Open Tues-Sun, May-Aug, 10am-5pm. 01255 503429. www.city2000.com/tl/harsoc

Ⓐ **Harwich Maritime Museum,** Low Lighthouse, Harwich Green, in a disused
Schools lighthouse, this small museum has specialised displays on the Royal Navy and commercial
shipping. Beware the almost vertical ladders between the floors! Open daily May-Aug
10am-5pm. 01255 503429. www.city2000.com/tl/harsoc

Ⓐ **Harwich Redoubt Fort.** An extremely well-preserved, circular, Napoleonic fort.
Schools Used in both World Wars. There are 11 guns on the battlements and various small displays
in the casemates. Open daily May-Aug 10am-5pm. Jan-Apr & Sept-Dec, Suns only 10am-
5pm. Closed Christmas. 01255 503429. www.city2000.com/tl/harsoc

ⓒ **Hedingham Castle,** Castle Hedingham, well sign posted from the A1017, is one of
Schools the best preserved Norman keeps in England. Set in pretty woodland, ideal for picnics and
walks, the castle has four splendid floors to explore. Open daily week before Easter-end
Oct, 10am-5pm. 01787 460261. www.information-britain.co.uk

Hollytrees Museum, High Street, **Colchester,** next to the Castle. See "Free Places"
chapter.

ⓒ **Ickworth House,** NT, near **Bury St Edmunds.** A children's guide is available for this
Schools fascinating house which is surrounded by gardens and a park with deer, vineyard, church,
canal and lake. There are waymarked walks, a family cycle route, woodland trim trail and
adventure playground. House open 24th Mar-28th Oct, Tues, Wed, Fri-Sun and Bank Hol
Mons, 1-5pm. Restaurant and shop open, 12-5pm. Garden open daily 10am-5pm, (4pm in
Winter), closed weekends Nov-Mar. Park open daily, all year, 7am-7pm. Closed 25th Dec.
01284 735270. www.nationaltrust.org.uk/ickworth

Ⓕ Schools **Ipswich Museum,** High Street. See "Free Places" chapter.
Open all year
Ⓑ **Ipswich Transport Museum,** Cobham Road, **Ipswich,** is the largest transport
Schools museum in the country devoted to items from just one town. It covers everything from
prams to double-decker trolleybuses. Special themed open days throughout the season.
Parties by arrangement. Open Apr-end Nov, Sun and Bank Hol Mons, 11am-4.30pm; School
hols, Mon-Fri, 1-4pm. 01473 715666. www.ipswichtransportmuseum.co.uk

Price Codes for a family of four: Ⓐ: less than £5   Ⓑ: £5-£10   ⓒ: £10-£15   Ⓓ: £15-£20   Ⓔ: £20-£30   Ⓖ: £30-£50   Ⓗ: Over £50   Ⓕ: Free
Map Ref: Grid square on Page 2 Map   Schools: Facilities available   ● Birthday parties

Historic Sites, Castles, Museums & Science Centres

B3 ⓓ / ⓔ Schools **Kentwell Hall,** Long Melford, is a mellow, red brick Tudor mansion surrounded by a broad moat. The gardens, grounds and Home Farm are ideal for youngsters. On certain weekends in the Summer, you can step back in time to the 16th century when the house is peopled by Tudors. Phone to confirm dates. Open daily, beg April-end Sept. 01787 310207. www.kentwell.co.uk

ⓐ Schools Open all year **Little Hall,** Market Place, Lavenham. Built in the 1390s, this ancient, timber-framed house is a gem. Delightfully furnished, with a beautiful walled garden. Open Wed, Thurs, Sat & Sun 2-5.30pm. Bank Hols 11am-5.30pm. Groups at other times, by arrangement. 01787 247179.

ⓑ Schools **Manor House Museum,** Honey Hill, Bury St Edmunds. This restored Georgian mansion houses a collection of beautiful clocks, watches, decorative art and costume. Children will enjoy doing the quiz and the ghost hunt! Open Tues, Weds, Sat & Sun, 10am-5pm, closed 25th, 26th Dec and Good Fri. 01284 757072. www.stedmundsbury.gov.uk/manorhouse

ⓑ Schools **Mechanical Music Museum and Bygones,** Blacksmith's Road, Cotton. A unique collection of musical instruments, including organs, street pianos, musical boxes and a mighty Wurlitzer. Many unusual items, all in working order and played while you visit. Open Jun-Sept, Suns, 2-5.30pm, or by arrangement for groups during the week. 1st Sun in Oct, Fair Organ Enthusiast Day, 10am-5pm. 01449 613876.

ⓒ Schools **Melford Hall,** NT, Long Melford, is a turreted brick Tudor mansion, little changed externally since 1578. A children's guide is available. Open 23rd Mar-30th Apr, weekends and Bank Hol Mon, Wed-Sun and Bank Hol Mon, May-Sept, 2-5.30pm. 1st Oct-3rd Nov, weekends only. 01787 880286. www.nationaltrust.org.uk

ⓓ Schools **Museum of East Anglian Life,** centrally situated in Stowmarket, is a busy 70 acre site full of interesting exhibits looking at local life, agriculture, crafts and industry. Fun activity days, demonstrations and special events are held during the Summer season. Open Apr-Oct, Mon-Sat, 10am-5pm, Sun, 11am-5pm. 01449 612229. www.suffolkcc.gov.uk/central/meal

ⓕ Schools Open all year **Natural History Museum,** All Saint's Church, Colchester, opposite the Castle. See "Free Places" chapter.

ⓑ Schools **Pakenham Water Mill,** near Bury St. Edmunds. This 18th century water mill has been fully restored by the Suffolk Building Preservation Trust. Frequent guided tours are given and there is a picnic area in the mill grounds. Enjoy a stroll along the river bank. Open Good Fri-end Sept, Weds, Sats & Suns and Bank Hols 2-5.30pm. Open for parties at other times by arrangement. 01359 230275.

ⓑ Schools **Paycockes,** NT, Coggeshall, off the A120. This timber-framed building dates back to the 16th century. It houses a display of fine lace and there is a lovely garden. Joint ticket available with Grange Barn. (Parking at Barn). Open 14th Apr-20th Oct, Tues, Thurs, Sun and Bank Hol Mons, 2-5.30pm (last admission 5pm). 01376 561305. www.nationaltrust.org.uk

ⓑ Schools **The Guildhall of Corpus Christi,** NT, Market Place, Lavenham, is an early 16th century timber-framed building housing displays on local history, farming industry, the woollen cloth trade and the railways. Children's guide available. There is a lovely walled garden and tearoom. Open Mar & Nov, Sat & Sun 11am-4pm; Apr, May and Oct, Wed-Sun 11am-5pm, Jun-Sept and Bank Hol Mons, daily 11am-5pm, closed Good Fri. 01787 247646. www.nationaltrust.org.uk

ⓕ Schools Open all year **Tymperleys Clock Museum,** Trinity Street, Colchester. See "Free Places" chapter.

ⓕ Schools Open all year **Beecroft Art Gallery,** Station Road, Westcliff. See "Free Places" chapter.

Price Codes for a family of four: Ⓐ: less than £5 Ⓑ: £5-£10 Ⓒ: £10-£15 Ⓓ: £15-£20 Ⓔ: £20-£30 Ⓖ: £30-£50 Ⓗ: Over £50 Ⓕ: Free
Map Ref: Grid square on Page 2 Map   Schools: Facilities available   🎈 Birthday parties

MAP REFS	PRICE CODES		

B4 — Ⓕ Schools **Bradwell Visitor Centre,** Bradwell-on-Sea, Southminster. See "Free Places" chapter.
Open all year

Ⓑ / Ⓕ Schools **Castle Point Transport Museum,** 105 Point Road, **Canvey Island.** Rides available at the Transport Show, 2nd Sun in Oct. Open at other times by arrangement for pre-booked parties. 01268 684272. See also "Free Places" chapter.

Ⓕ Schools **Central Museum,** Victoria Avenue, **Southend.** See "Free Places" chapter.
Open all year

Ⓑ Schools **Central Museum Planetarium,** Victoria Avenue, **Southend,** is a traditional planetarium housed in the Central Museum. Performances at 11am, 2 & 4pm. Open Wed-Sat. Closed Bank Hols. 01702 434449. www.southendmuseums.co.uk
Open all year

Ⓒ Schools 🍎 **Mangapps Farm Railway Museum,** Southminster Road, **Burnham-on-Crouch,** has undercover displays of steam and diesel memorabilia and a working three-quarter mile railway line. Special events days are held during the year including the fantastic Thomas Tank event. Open weekends & Bank Hols, 1-5pm, daily Easter fortnight & Aug, 1-5pm. Closed Jan. 01621 784898. www.mangapps.co.uk

Ⓐ Schools **Pier Museum,** **Southend,** accessed from Southend Pier railway, shore end station. This small museum houses a varied and interesting collection charting the history of the longest pier in the world from 1830 to the present day. Open beg May-end Oct, Tues, Wed, Sat & Sun, 11am-5pm, peak times 6pm. 01702 614553/611214.

Ⓕ Schools **Prittlewell Priory Museum,** Priory Park, Victoria Avenue, **Southend.** See "Free Places" chapter.
Open all year

Ⓕ Schools **Southchurch Hall,** Park Lane, **Southend.** See "Free Places" chapter.
Open all year

C1 — Ⓑ Schools **Happisburgh Lighthouse.** Climb the 112 steps of this red-and-white striped coastal landmark for spectacular views, plus an informative historical guide. Not for vertigo sufferers or children under 8. Open end of May-end Sept, Sun 2.30-4.30pm. 01692 650803.

Ⓐ **Horsey Windpump,** NT, near **Horsey.** Clamber up the steep wooden stairs of this early 20th century drainage pump for good views of the Broads. Then take a stroll along the river or to the beach. Open daily Apr-Sept, 11am-5pm. 01493 393904. www.nationaltrust.org.uk

Ⓐ Schools **Museum of the Broads,** The Staithe, **Stalham.** A children's hands-on activity corner brings to life the story of the history of the Broads. Quiz sheets and activities for children. Open Easter-31st Oct, Mon-Fri, 11am-5pm, daily during school hols. 01692 581681. www.whiteswan.u-net.com

Ⓐ Schools **Norfolk Motor Cycle Museum,** Railway Yard, **North Walsham.** The collection has a wide range of motor cycles dating from 1920 to 1960. Open daily Apr-Oct, 10am-4.30pm, Mon-Sat during Winter. Closed 24th Dec-2nd Jan. 01692 406366.

Ⓑ Schools **RAF Air Defence Radar Museum,** RAF Neatishead, off A1062 near **Horning.** Housed in the original 1942 Operations Building, this museum tells the story of RADAR from its conception to modern computer technology. Open Tues and Thurs, 4th Apr-30th Sept, 10am-5pm (last admissions 3pm); open 2nd Sat of each month throughout the year. 01692 633309. www.neatishead.raf.mod.uk
Open all year

Ⓑ Schools **Sutton Windmill and Broads Museum,** **Sutton,** off A149 near Stalham. Climb Britain's tallest windmill and enjoy fine views of surrounding countryside and coast. The adjoining museum has a wealth of exhibits, telling the story of social life in the area. Open daily, Easter-Sept, 10am-5.30pm. 01692 581195.

Price Codes for a family of four: Ⓐ: less than £5 Ⓑ: £5-£10 Ⓒ: £10-£15 Ⓓ: £15-£20 Ⓔ: £20-£30 Ⓖ: £30-£50 Ⓗ: Over £50 Ⓕ: Free
Map Ref: Grid square on Page 2 Map   Schools: Facilities available   🍎 Birthday parties

Historic Sites, Castles, Museums & Science Centres

C2

Ⓐ Schools **Berney Arms Windmill,** EH, Berney Arms Marshes, **Great Yarmouth**. Inaccessible by car, this Norfolk marshmill with 7 floors houses an exhibition on windmills. Access is by footpath or river. Open daily Apr-Oct, 9am-1pm and 2-5pm. 01493 700605. Schools, 01223 582700.

Ⓒ Schools **Caister Castle Car Collection,** Caister-on-Sea, off the A1064, has a vast collection of fine and rare veteran, vintage, classic, sports and touring automobiles and motorcycles. Also early bicycles, horse-drawn vehicles, baby carriages and pedal cars. Under-5s Ⓕ. Open Sun-Fri, mid-May-27th Sept, 10am-4.30pm. 01572 787251.

Ⓕ Schools **Dunwich Museum,** St James Street. See "Free Places" chapter.

Ⓐ Schools **Dunwich Underwater Exploration Exhibition,** Orford Craft Shop, **Orford**, shows the progress being made in the underwater exploration of the "city that sunk beneath the sea". Open daily, 11am-5pm. Closed Christmas. 01394 450678.

Ⓒ Schools **East Anglia Transport Museum,** Carlton Colville, near **Lowestoft** on B1384, is a must for tram, bus and trolley-bus lovers. Clamber aboard and take a short ride. Entry price includes rides. Open Good Fri, Easter Sat, 2-5pm, Sun & Mon, 11am-5.30pm, then Suns and Bank Hols, May-Sept, 11am-5.30pm. Also Jun-Sept, Weds & Sats 2-5pm; Aug, Mon-Fri, 2-5pm. Last entry 1 hour before closing. 01502 518459.

Ⓐ Schools **Elizabethan House Museum,** NT, 4 South Quay, **Great Yarmouth**. Built in 1596, each room depicts life in a different century, while the activity packed Toy Room is of special interest to children. During the school holidays, there are family events on the 1st Mon of the month. Open beg Apr-25th Oct, Mon-Fri, 10am-5pm; Sat and Sun, 1.15-5pm. 01493 745526. www.nationaltrust.org.uk

Ⓕ Schools **Laxfield and District Museum,** Guildhall, High Street. See "Free Places" chapter.

Ⓐ Schools **Lowestoft and East Suffolk Maritime Museum,** Sparrow's Nest Park, Whapload Road. This small but packed museum tells the story of the Lowestoft fishing fleets from sail to steam and diesel. Also exhibitions on lifeboats, the Royal Navy and a full sized replica of the cabin of a steam drifter. Open Easter weekend and daily May-beg Oct, 10am-5pm. Groups at other times. 01502 561963/511260.

Ⓕ Schools **Lowestoft Museum,** Nicholas Everitt Park. See "Free Places" chapter.

Ⓐ Schools **Maritime Museum,** 25 Marine Parade, **Great Yarmouth**. From an Egyptian mummified hand to an oar that stands three stories tall, this is a fascinating mix of interesting artefacts, mostly thematically arranged. Test your observational skills with a not-so-easy family quiz. Open Easter fortnight, Sun-Fri 10am-5pm; closed Good Fri and Sat; open Sun-Fri 6th May-28th Sept, 10am-5pm. 01493 842267. www.norfolk.gov.uk/tourism/museums

Ⓕ Schools **Norfolk and Suffolk Aviation Museum,** Flixton. See "Free Places" chapter.

Ⓑ Schools **Norfolk Nelson Museum,** 26 South Quay, **Great Yarmouth**. A new museum due to open Summer 2002. Learn about the life and history of Nelson and experience for yourself the rigours of life at sea. Ring for more details. 01603 713488. www.nelson-museum.co.uk

Ⓑ Schools Open all year 🎈 **Pottery Workshops,** 18/19 Trinity Place, off Blackfriars Road, **Great Yarmouth**. Full working pottery with herring smoking museum, made from 300 year-old shipwreck timbers. Children can pull the bucket up from the ancient well, take part in a quiz and make their own animals (small extra charge). Refreshments available. Open Mon-Fri 9.30am-12.15pm, 1.30-4.15pm (Sat by special arrangement); closed Christmas period. 01493 850585.

Price Codes for a family of four: Ⓐ: less than £5 Ⓑ: £5-£10 Ⓒ: £10-£15 Ⓓ: £15-£20 Ⓔ: £20-£30 Ⓖ: £30-£50 Ⓗ: Over £50 Ⓕ: Free
Map Ref: Grid square on Page 2 Map   Schools: Facilities available   🎈 Birthday parties

MAP REFS	PRICE CODES		
C2	Ⓑ Schools	**Row 111 Houses/Old Merchant's House,** EH, South Quay, **Great Yarmouth.** The sole remaining 17th century town house, of significant local architectural interest, typical of its day. Open daily Apr-Oct, 10am-5pm (closed 1-2pm); entry by hourly guided tour only. 01493 857900. Schools, 01223 582700. www.english-heritage.org.uk	
	Ⓒ Schools	**Somerleyton Hall and Gardens,** Somerleyton, near Lowestoft. Children and parents alike will love getting lost in the maze. There's a dolls' house, and look out for the Polar Bears! Picnic area and gift shop. Open Easter Sun-end Sept, Sun, Thurs & Bank Hols 1-5pm; also Tues & Wed in Jul & Aug. Gardens and tearoom from 12.30-5.30pm. 01502 730224. www.somerleyton.co.uk	
	Ⓕ	**Southwold Museum,** Bartholomew Green. See "Free Places" chapter.	
	Ⓑ / Ⓕ Schools	**Strumpshaw Steam Museum,** Strumpshaw. Follow signs off A47. An Aladdin's Cave of steam engines and farm machinery of interest to all ages. Take a ride on the 1930s fairground carousel and the narrow gauge railway. Free admission on Suns. Open 2nd Jul-2nd Oct, Sun-Fri, 11am-4pm. 01603 714535.	
	Ⓐ Schools	**Tollhouse Museum,** South Quay, **Great Yarmouth.** Visit the dungeons and see the Victorian prisoners locked in their cells, in this, one of the oldest civic buildings in England. Open Jun-end Sept, Mon-Fri, 10am-5pm, Sat and Sun, 1.15-5pm. 01493 745526. www.norfolk.gov.uk/tourism/museums	
C3	Ⓑ Schools Open all year	**Framlingham Castle,** EH, is a real castle. Walking round the rampart walls is a highlight of any visit here. Audio guide available. A room in the castle houses the Lanman Museum of local history. Open daily, 10am-6pm, 4pm in Winter. Closed 25th-26th Dec. 01728 724189. Education Service, 01223 582715.	
	Ⓑ Schools	**Long Shop Museum,** Main Street, **Leiston.** This listed building, which originally housed the first ever production line, is now the largest industrial museum in East Anglia. Gleaming steam engines and an immense variety of products testify to Victorian genius. Plenty to keep inquisitive youngsters interested. Open Apr-Oct, daily, 10am-5pm, 11am opening Suns. 01728 832189.	
	Ⓑ Schools Open all year	**Orford Castle.** EH. This 12th century keep dominates the surrounding creeks and marshes. The climb up is worth it for the wonderful views. Open daily, 10am-6pm, Apr-Sept, Wed-Sun, 10am-1pm, 2-6pm (5pm, Oct) Nov-Mar. Closed Christmas. 01394 450472. Education Service, 01223 582715.	
	Ⓑ Schools	**Saxtead Green Post Mill.** EH. Striking 18th century windmill in perfect working order. Its wooden staircase rotates with the body of the mill making it an exciting place to visit. Free audio tour (takes 1 hour). Open Apr-Oct, Mon-Sat, 10am-6pm (5pm Oct), closed 1-2pm. 01728 685789. Education 01223 582715 (pre-booked school parties - free). www.english-heritage.org.uk	
	Ⓐ Schools	**Suffolk Horse Museum,** Market Hill, **Woodbridge.** An award-winning, small but busy museum devoted to the history of the Suffolk Punch breed of horse. Displays include an excellent video, a blacksmith's shop, harness maker's workshop, horseman's kitchen and 1930s office as well as paintings, photographs and silver. Open daily Easter Mon-end Sept, 2-5pm. 01394 380643. www.woodbridgeweb.co.uk	
	Ⓐ Schools	**Woodbridge Museum,** Market Hill. A small museum with a permanent exhibition on the Anglo-Saxon burial sites at Burrow Hill and Sutton Hoo and changing exhibitions which reflect the history and life of Woodbridge. Open Easter-end Sept, Thurs-Sat, 10am-4pm, Sun 2.30-4.30pm. Summer school hols and Oct half-term also open Mon & Tues, 10am-4pm. 01394 380502. www.woodbridgeweb.co.uk	
	Ⓐ Schools	**Woodbridge Tide Mill.** An attractive 18th century building housing a rare tide-driven mill complete with restored machinery and fun working model. Open Easter weekend, then daily, May-Sept, Apr & Oct weekends only, 11am-5pm. Open all year for school visits (small charge). 01473 626618. www.woodbridgeweb.co.uk	

Price Codes for a family of four: Ⓐ: less than £5 Ⓑ: £5-£10 Ⓒ: £10-£15 Ⓓ: £15-£20 Ⓔ: £20-£30 Ⓖ: £30-£50 Ⓗ: Over £50 Ⓕ: Free
Map Ref: Grid square on Page 2 Map   Schools: Facilities available   🎈 Birthday parties

Farms, Wildlife & Nature Parks

Flora and fauna at its best for you to enjoy.

MAP REFS	PRICE CODES	
A1	Ⓑ Schools	**Anville Falconry,** Waterlow Rd, **Terrington St Clement.** This newly opened centre is devoted to the rescue and conservation of birds of prey and other wildlife. There are falconry displays twice daily and lessons by appointment. Open daily, 1st Apr-24th Dec, 9am-5pm. 01553 829829.
	Ⓑ Schools Open all year	**The Green Quay,** Marriotts Warehouse, South Quay, **King's Lynn.** Explore the Wash and its wildlife at this interactive discovery centre, suitable for all ages. Phone for information on a regular programme of events. Open daily, 10am-5pm. 01553 818500. www.thegreenquay.co
	Ⓓ Schools Open all year 🎈	**Hunstanton Sea Life and Marine Sanctuary,** Southern Promenade. Explore the hidden depths of the marine world and encounter, at close hand, creatures such as sharks, crabs, starfish and eels. Open daily 10am-4.30pm (earlier during Winter months; please phone for details); closed 25th Dec. 01485 533576. www.sealife.co.uk
	Ⓒ Schools Open all year 🎈	**Park Farm, Snettisham** (near to the church) provides both in and outdoor entertainment. From safari tours (additional charge), farm trails and pony rides to pot throwing, craft and leather centres, this attraction appeals to all ages. Tea room and picnic facilities. Open daily, Feb-Oct, 10am-5pm (or dusk, if earlier); Nov-Jan, 10am-4pm; closed 24th Dec-4th Jan. 01485 542472.
	Ⓕ Open all year	**Snettisham Coastal Park,** off A149 near **Snettisham.** See "Free Places" chapter.
	Ⓕ Open all year	**Titchwell Marsh,** RSPB, off A149 W of **Brancaster.** See "Free Places" chapter.
A2	Ⓑ Schools Open all year	**Wildfowl and Wetlands Trust,** Hundred Foot Bank, **Welney.** Discover the unique fenland landscape and its wildlife. Phone for details of holiday family activities (except Christmas). Pond-dipping throughout the Summer. In Winter you can watch hundreds of wild birds being fed by floodlight (Nov-Feb, Wed-Sun, 6.30pm). Open daily, 10am-5pm; closed 25th Dec. 01353 860711. www.wwt.org.uk
A3	Ⓑ Schools Open all year	**Botanic Gardens,** Bateman Street, **Cambridge.** Enjoy a rich variety of plants in landscaped gardens and glasshouses. There is a picnic area. Annual family passes available. Open daily 10am-dusk (Winter), 6pm (Summer). Closed Christmas. 01223 336265. www.botanic.cam.ac.uk
	Ⓑ Schools 🎈	**Boydell's Farm,** Wethersfield, near Braintree on B1053, is a small dairy farm where you can watch sheep and cows being milked and admire lots of other animals. Fascinating observation beehive. Open Easter-30th Sept, Fri, Sat and Sun (daily in school hols), 2-5pm. 01371 850481. members.farmline.com/boydells
	Ⓐ Schools Open all year	**Fowlmere Nature Reserve,** RSPB, off A10 near **Shepreth,** has a nature trail and four hides (free to members). Field teaching scheme linked to National Curriculum includes excellent pond dipping. Open daily. 01763 208978. Education Service 01767 650834.
	Ⓕ Schools Open all year	**Hinchingbrooke Country Park,** Brampton Road, **Huntingdon.** See "Free Places" chapter.

Price Codes for a family of four: Ⓐ: less than £5   Ⓑ: £5-£10   Ⓒ: £10-£15   Ⓓ: £15-£20   Ⓔ: £20-£30   Ⓖ: £30-£50   Ⓗ: Over £50   Ⓕ: Free
Map Ref: Grid square on Page 2 Map   Schools: Facilities available   🎈 Birthday parties

You lookin' at me?

Come and see Rana at Shepreth Wildlife Park, He's waiting!

Free guide book with this advert

Open 7 days 10am – 6pm
01763 26 22 26
www.SheprethWildlifePark.co.uk

Just 6 miles south of Cambridge on the A10

Farms, Wildlife & Nature Parks

MAP REFS: A3

PRICE CODES

Ⓓ Schools Open all year
Linton Zoo, just off the A1307, 10 miles SE of **Cambridge**, is set in 16 acres of beautiful gardens and provides a breeding centre for many threatened animals, birds and reptiles. On Special Days there are animal encounters, Zebra keeper talk, Tapir feed and keeper talk and flying displays weekends and school hols (weather permitting). Covered education area. Open daily, except 25th Dec, 10am-6pm (dusk in Winter). 01223 891308.

Ⓒ Schools Open all year
Mole Hall Wildlife Park, Widdington, near Saffron Walden, covers some 20 acres with lovely woodland and waterside paths. A wide variety of animals include favourites like otters, chimps, red squirrels, wallabies, flamingos, owls, and Formosan Sika deer, which are extinct in the wild. A great attraction during the Summer is the Butterfly Pavilion housing a beautiful collection of these colourful creatures in tropical surroundings, and parents and children alike will have fun getting lost in the gigantic Maize Maze. Visit the website for details of a new theme for 2002. School parties are particularly well catered for, with work sheets and teachers' packs available free from the website. Schools/Groups at discount prices. Open daily, 10.30am-6pm (or dusk in Winter). Butterfly House open Easter-end Oct and Maize Maze, late Jul-Sept. 01799 540400. www.molehall.co.uk (See Advert page 65.)

Ⓑ Schools 🎂
National Horseracing Museum, 99 High Street, **Newmarket**, can arrange fascinating tours of the racecourse, training grounds and studs. Open Easter-end Oct, Tues-Sun, 10am-5pm, also Mons, Jul & Aug and all Bank Hols. (See "Historic Sites" chapter.) 01638 667333. www.nhrm.co.uk

Ⓓ Schools Open all year 🎂
Shepreth Wildlife Park, Willers Mill, Station Rd, **Shepreth**, is home to many species which have been donated or rescued, including tigers, puma, lynx, wolves, tropical birds, monkeys, raccoons and otters. Get closer to the animals in the petting field, where children can feed the goats, ponies, sheep and deer. Wander through the Tropical Pavilion, the Reptile House or hand feed the giant carp. Visit Water World and Bug City, which house a fascinating selection from around the world. Don't miss the leaf cutting ants, giant millipedes, tarantulas, piranhas, sturgeon, baby alligator or any of the many other amazing creatures on view. There are also hands-on sessions throughout the day, plus cafe facilities and an adventure playground. Highly recommended. Open daily, 10am-6pm (dusk in Winter). 09066 800031 (25p/min). www.sheprethwildlifepark.co.uk (See Advert page 58.)

Ⓑ Schools Open all year
The Raptor Foundation, The Heath, St Ives Road, **Woodhurst**, on B1040 to Somersham. Set in 30 acres and home to over 300 raptors, this Bird of Prey Sanctuary and Hospital is a unique and exciting place to meet and learn about owls, falcons, hawks and buzzards. Flying displays as posted. Tearoom, gift shop, exhibition room and guided tours. Open daily, 10.30am-5pm. Closed 25th Dec & 1st Jan. 01487 741140. www.homepages.tesco.net/~raptor.foundation

Ⓒ Schools 🎂
Wimpole Home Farm, NT, **Arrington**, N of Royston, off the A603, covers 350 acres within the grounds of Wimpole Hall and Park. There are lots of animals to see in the farmyard, a special children's corner with a picnic area and adventure playground. Lambing weekends in Apr. Open 23rd Mar-3rd Nov, Tues-Thurs, Sat & Sun, and Bank Hols, 10.30am-5pm (Fri in Jul & Aug). 9th Nov-16th Mar, Sat & Sun 11am-4pm. 01223 207257. www.wimpole.org (See also "Historic Sites" chapter.)

Ⓕ Schools Open all year
Wood Green Animal Shelters, Chishill Road, **Heydon**, near Royston. See "Free Places" chapter.

Ⓕ Schools Open all year 🎂
Wood Green Animal Shelters, King's Bush Farm, **Godmanchester**, (just off A14). See "Free Places" chapter.

MAP REFS: A4

Ⓐ Schools Open all year 🎂
Ada Cole Memorial Stables, Broadley Common, on the B181 between Harlow and Epping, is a haven for rescued horses, ponies, donkeys and mules. Information Centre and shop. Open daily, Apr-Oct, 2-5pm, Nov-Mar, 2-4pm. Closed 25th Dec & 1st Jan. 01992 892133. www.adacolestables.sagenet.co.uk

---

Price Codes for a family of four: Ⓐ: less than £5 Ⓑ: £5-£10 Ⓒ: £10-£15 Ⓓ: £15-£20 Ⓔ: £20-£30 Ⓖ: £30-£50 Ⓗ: Over £50 Ⓕ: Free
Map Ref: Grid square on Page 2 Map   Schools: Facilities available   ● Birthday parties

| MAP REFS | PRICE CODES |

A4

Ⓑ Schools 🎈 **Barleylands Farm and Museum,** Barleylands Road, **Billericay**, offers a fascinating glimpse into life on a modern working farm. There are ducks, sheep, rabbits, goats, ponies, cows, pigs, guinea-fowl, turkeys, quail and chickens to see along the Farm Trail. Open daily, 10am-5pm, Mar-Oct. 01268 532253/290229. (See "Historic Sites" chapter.)

Ⓒ Schools Open all year 🎈 **Basildon Zoo,** London Road, **Vange**, houses a collection of birds and animals. Open daily, 10am-5pm; last admission 4pm, earlier in Winter. Closed 25th-26th Dec. 01268 553985.

Ⓒ Schools Open all year 🎈 **Hayes Hill Farm & Holyfield Hall Farm,** Waltham Abbey, part of the Lee Valley Regional Park, situated in a beautiful, secluded valley off Stubbins Hall Lane, Crooked Mile. Traditional style farms with lots of animals to see including milking every day at 2.45pm. Children's adventure play area. Open weekdays, 10am-4.30pm, weekends & Bank Hols, 10am-6pm.. 01992 892781. www.leevalleypark.org.uk

Ⓑ Schools Open all year 🎈 **Hobbs Cross Open Farm,** Theydon Garnon, near Epping, is a real working livestock farm. Children will particularly enjoy seeing, feeding and touching the animals. There is a licenced restaurant, adventure playground, tractor raceway, playbarn and toddlers room. (See also "Theme Parks & Play Parks" chapter.) Guided tours for groups. Open daily, 9am-6pm, 5pm weekdays in Winter. Closed Mons in Winter. 01992 814764.

Ⓕ Schools Open all year **Lee Valley Park Information Centre,** Abbey Gardens at **Waltham Abbey**. See "Free Places" chapter.

Ⓑ Schools Open all year 🎈 **Old MacDonalds Educational Farm Park,** South Weald, Brentwood, 5 mins A12/M25, Jn 28, is a well-tended show farm set in 17 acres of pasture and woodland. It is home to a large selection of Native Rare Breed sheep, pigs, cattle and poultry and there is a wonderful rabbitry, displaying many breeds from tiny Dwarfs to the large British Giants. See the magnificent owls, or watch at close quarters the small herd of fallow deer. Spend time watching the farm's breeding colony of Red Squirrels or meet Nipper and Cuddles the otters. Children will love meeting the chipmunks, shire horses, goats, ferrets and host of other animals and birds and finding out all about them from the very informative labelling system. The park is very pushchair and wheelchair friendly with hard paths, play area, café, gift shop, picnic areas, disabled toilets and excellent wash facilities. Open daily, 10am-6pm, dusk in Winter. Closed 25th-26th Dec. 01277 375177. www.oldmacdonaldsfarm.org.uk (See Advert page 65.)

Paradise Wildlife Park, White Stubbs Lane, **Broxbourne**, just over the border into Herts. See "Places to Go Outside the Area" chapter and Advert page 70.

B1

Ⓕ Open all year **Blakeney Point,** NT. Access from Cley beach or by ferry from Morston and Blakeney. See "Free Places" chapter.

Schools **Brancaster Millennium Activity Centre,** NT, Dial House, **Brancaster Staithe**, on A149 between Wells and Hunstanton. This field study centre offers residential courses for schools on bird watching, coastal processes, woodlands, saltmarshes, orienteering, sailing, cycling, kayaking and "Family Fun" weeks in Aug. 01485 210719.

Ⓑ Open all year **Cley Marshes,** NWT, **Cley-next-the-Sea**. This coastal nature reserve attracts many migrant and wading birds. Excellent, thatched birdwatching hides. Visitor and information centre overlooks the reserve. Wildlife gift shop. Visitor centre open Tues-Sun, Apr-Oct, 10am-5pm. 01263 740008. www.wildlifetrust.org.uk/norfolk

Ⓕ Schools Open all year **Holt Country Park,** on B1149 just S of **Holt**. See "Free Places" chapter.

Ⓑ Schools 🎈 **Mannington Gardens & Countryside,** signposted off B1149 between Norwich and Holt, offers beautiful gardens, countryside and lake surrounding a medieval moated manor house. There is a schools programme and nature discovery days for children during the holidays. Gardens open Sun, May-Sept, 12-5pm; also Wed-Fri, Jun-Aug, 11am-5pm. Countryside walks open all year (small car park fee). 01263 584175.

Price Codes for a family of four: Ⓐ: less than £5 Ⓑ: £5-£10 Ⓒ: £10-£15 Ⓓ: £15-£20 Ⓔ: £20-£30 Ⓖ: £30-£50 Ⓗ: Over £50 Ⓕ: Free
Map Ref: Grid square on Page 2 Map   Schools: Facilities available   🎈 Birthday parties

Farms, Wildlife & Nature Parks

B1

(D) Schools — **Norfolk Shire Horse Centre,** West Runton Stables, **West Runton.** Home to a wide variety of Heavy Horse breeds and small animals, there are regular harnessing demonstrations and live animal parades. Large display of bygone machines, carts, wagons and gipsy caravans. Attractions include free cart rides, a children's farm and the adjoining **West Runton Riding Stables.** Picnic facilities, café and souvenir shop. Open 24th Mar-27th Oct, Sun-Fri, 10am-5pm; daily, Aug and Bank Hols Sats. 01263 837339. www.norfolk-shirehorse-centre.co.uk

(C) Schools — **Norfolk Wildlife Centre and Country Park,** Great **Witchingham,** 12 miles NW of Norwich, off the A1067, is home to a wide collection of British and European wildlife. See the model farm, pet's corner, and clear-water carp pool. Children will enjoy the challenge of the commando and adventure play areas. Picnic, café and gift shop. Open daily 1st Apr-31st Oct, 10am-6pm, Sat, Sun and school hols during Winter. 01603 872274. www.norfolkwildlife.co.uk

(C) Schools Open all year — **Pensthorpe Waterfowl Park,** Fakenham, on A1067 Norwich to Fakenham Road. 200 acres of lakes, woodland and meadows in which to observe this collection of endangered and exotic waterbirds. Children's play area and Observation and Exhibition Galleries. Open daily, 10am-5pm, Apr-Dec. Closed 25th Dec. Sat, Sun only, Jan-Mar. 01328 851465.

(B) Schools Park open all year — **Wolterton Hall and Park,** Erpingham, signposted off A140 Norwich-Cromer Road. A beautiful Georgian house with lake and parkland. Permanent orienteering course and children's adventure playground. Special events (see local press for details). Hall open for tours Apr-Oct, Fri, 2-5pm (last entry 4pm). Park open daily for walks (small car park charge.) 01263 584175.

B2

(E) Schools Open all year — **Banham Zoo,** just in Norfolk signposted from the A11 and A140, **Attleborough** is set in over 35 acres of countryside and is home to over 1000 animals, birds and reptiles. Prices reduced out of season. Open daily, Apr-Jun, Oct, 10am-5pm. Jul-Sept, 10am-5.30pm. Nov-Mar 10am-4pm. Closed 24th-25th Dec. 01953 887771. www.banhamzoo.co.uk

(B) Schools — **Hillside Animal Sanctuary,** Hill Top Farm, Hall Lane, **Frettenham.** 800 rescued farm animals reside here, from cows, pigs, sheep, horses, ponies, donkeys and many others. The sanctuary was founded to help animals which suffered from the intensive farming industry. Open Easter-Oct, Sun and Bank Hol Mons, 1-5pm, Mons Jul-Aug. 01603 891227. www.hillside.org.uk

(F) — **International League for the Protection of Horses,** Overa House Farm, **Larling.** See "Free Places" chapter.

(F) Schools — **Ranworth Broad,** NWT, off B1140 Norwich to Acle Road. See "Free Places" chapter.

(F) Schools Open all year — **Redgrave and Lopham Fen,** Low Common, **South Lopham,** near Diss. See "Free Places" chapter.

(C) Schools — **Roots of Norfolk at Gressenhall - Norfolk Rural Life Museum,** Gressenhall. Part of the museum, Union Farm is run as a typical 1920s farm, worked by heavy horses and stocked with rare breeds of sheep, pigs and cows - a delight in the Spring when the young animals are born. Tour the site by horse- or tractor-drawn cart ride. Open daily, 24th Mar-3rd Nov, 10am-5pm. 01362 860563. (See also "Historic Sites" chapter.) www.norfolk.gov.uk/tourism/museums

(D) Schools — **Tropical Butterfly World,** Great **Ellingham.** See multi-coloured butterflies, spectacular moths and large furry caterpillars, and you'll feel you've travelled to another part of the world. Visit the bird/animal park, the giant maize maze (Summer) and the conservation walk. Open 1st Mar-mid Nov, Mon-Sat, 9am-6pm, Sun 10.30am-5pm. 01953 453175.

Price Codes for a family of four: (A): less than £5 (B): £5-£10 (C): £10-£15 (D): £15-£20 (E): £20-£30 (G): £30-£50 (H): Over £50 (F): Free
Map Ref: Grid square on Page 2 Map   Schools: Facilities available   ● Birthday parties

MAP REFS	PRICE CODES

B2 — (F) Schools, Open all year — **Thetford Forest Park.** See "Free Places" chapter.

B3 — (F) Schools, Open all year — **Abberton Reservoir Visitor Centre,** 6 miles SW of Colchester on B1026. See "Free Places" chapter.

(C) Schools — **Baylham House Rare Breeds Farm, Baylham,** off B1113, is home to many rare breeds including the friendly Maori pigs from New Zealand called Kune Kunes. Gifts and light refreshments are available in the Visitor Centre. Open daily, Easter-end Sept, 11am-5pm; closed Mon except Bank Hols and Oct half term. 01473 830264. www.baylham-house-farm.co.uk

(F) Schools — **Bradfield Woods,** Felsham Rd, **Bradfield St. George.** See "Free Places" chapter.

(E) Schools, Open all year — **Colchester Zoo,** Stanway, just S of Colchester, has nearly 200 endangered and exotic species set in 40 acres of parkland. Daily presentations and animal displays are educational. There is a soft play area and "Spirit of Africa" elephant kingdom. Open daily, except 25th Dec, from 9.30am. Last admission 5.30pm in Summer, one hour before dusk in Winter. 01206 331292. www.colchester-zoo.co.uk

(F) Schools, Open all year — **The Fingringhoe Centre.** See "Free Places" chapter.

(B) Schools — **Gifford's Hall Vineyard, Hartest,** is signposted off A134. Wander through the flower meadows, enjoying sweet peas in bloom from May to September, or take a free ride around the vineyard on the Grape Express. Enjoy meeting the rare breed pigs and sheep, feed the chickens and admire the peacocks. Children will love the play area. Open daily Easter-end Sept, 11am-6pm. 01284 830464. www.giffordshall.co.uk

(B) Schools — **Layer Marney Tower,** signposted off B1022, S of **Colchester,** has a rare breed farm within the grounds with cows, pigs, sheep, goats and deer. You can also climb to the top of the tallest Tudor Gatehouse in Britain. Open Easter-early Oct, daily, except Sats, 12-5pm. Bank Hols, 11am-6pm. 01206 330784. www.layermarneytower.co.uk

(A) Schools, Open all year — **Marks Hall Estate and Arboretum, Coggeshall.** This beautiful estate dates back to the Domesday Book. Explore over 300 acres of woodland via waymarked trails. The Visitor Centre has a gift shop and tea room. Visitor Centre and Arboretum open Easter-end Oct, Tues-Sun and Bank Hols, 10.30am-5pm (Winter weekends 10.30am-dusk). The Woodland Walks and picnic area are open daily all year. 01376 563796.

(B) Schools, Open all year — **Mistley Park Animal Rescue and Environmental Centre, Mistley,** near Manningtree, is home to over 2000 rescued farm and domestic animals including horses, goats, sheep, rabbits, guinea pigs and more. Children can feed, touch and make friends with the animals. At certain times, pony rides are also offered. There is a lovely freshwater lake, tea room and picnic tables. Open Easter-end Oct, 10am-dusk, weekends in Winter. 01206 396483.

(C) Schools, Open all year — **Suffolk Owl Sanctuary** at **Stonham Barns,** on A1120 off A140 Ipswich to Norwich Road. See hawks, falcons, owls, buzzards, red kites, vultures and a steppe eagle with spectacular flying displays, weather permitting. Red Squirrel conservation colony, nature walk with wild bird hides, toddler play area with sandpit and restaurant. Open daily, 10am-5pm. 01449 711425. www.owl-help.org.uk

B4 — (B) Schools — **Jakapeni Rare Breed Farm,** Burlington Gardens, **Hullbridge,** is a working organic smallholding where you can see rare breed animals and poultry. Enjoy the pets' corner, picnic area and country walks. Open Easter Sun-25th Oct, Suns and Bank Hols, 10.30am-5.30pm. Weekdays by appointment. 01702 232394.

(C) Schools, Open all year — **Marsh Farm, South Woodham Ferrers,** is part of Essex County Council. A taxi-service (charged) links Woodham Ferrers station with Marsh Farm. Motorists should follow the brown tourists signs for "Open Farm and Country Park". The park includes a

Price Codes for a family of four: (A): less than £5 (B): £5-£10 (C): £10-£15 (D): £15-£20 (E): £20-£30 (G): £30-£50 (H): Over £50 (F): Free
Map Ref: Grid square on Page 2 Map   Schools: Facilities available   ● Birthday parties

Farms, Wildlife & Nature Parks

B4 farm trail and a large nature reserve with riverside walks and picnic areas (see "Free Places" chapter). The timber-framed Visitors Centre houses a well stocked gift shop and tea-rooms. As you walk round the farm trail the children will enjoy feeding the animals and you can learn about the livestock through fun exhibits and farming games. There is also an indoor soft play area, adventure play area, pet's corner, walk-in animal paddocks and a chicken run. New heated classroom for children's craft activities. Regular weekend and holiday activities include pony rides, tractor trailer rides, pet feeding, "meet a stockman" and bouncy castle (weather permitting). Guided tours, birthday parties and groups, by arrangement. Open daily mid Feb-end Oct, 10am-4.30pm (5.50pm weekends, Bank Hols and Summer Hols). Weekends only, Nov-mid Dec. For exact dates and details of events call 01245 324191 or visit www.marshfarmcountrypark.co.uk (See Advert outside back cover.)

(D) **Sea Life Adventure,** Eastern Esplanade, **Southend.** Journey beneath the ocean waves and discover amazing sea creatures. Attractions include a dramatic walk-through tunnel and many hi-tech displays, providing some fishy close encounters! Little Tikes activity centre, restaurant and gift shop. Open daily Mar-Sept 10am-5pm, Oct-Feb, Mon-Fri 11am-3pm, weekends and School hols 10am-5pm. Closed 25th Dec. 01702 601834. www.sealifeadventure.co.uk
Schools
Open all year

(B) **Walton Hall Farm Museum,** Linford, near **Stanford-le-Hope.** Browse at the memorabilia and look back in time at the representations of Edwardian / Victorian nurseries. Visit the working reconstruction of a village bakery. There are barbecue areas, snack bar, souvenir shop and children's play area. Open Thurs-Sun, 10am-5pm; other times by arrangement; closed from Christmas until a week before Easter. Open school hols. 01375 671874.
Schools

C1 (F) **Bacton Wood,** off B1150 near **North Walsham.** See "Free Places" chapter.
Open all year

(A) **Hickling Broad Nature Reserve,** NWT, off A149, 4 miles south of **Stalham.** Explore the boardwalk nature trails through reedbeds and open water and take a guided wildlife boat trail on this largest and wildest of the Norfolk Broads. Children under 16 (F). Refreshments, picnic site and wildlife gift shop. Visitor centre open daily, Apr-Sept, 10am-5pm. 01692 598276. School groups contact 01603 625540.
Schools
Open all year

(F) Schools **Toad Hole Cottage,** BA, How Hill, **Ludham.** See "Free Places" chapter.

(B) **Wroxham Barns,** Tunstead Road, **Hoveton.** A cornucopia of 18th century barns and craft workshops. The Junior Farm is a delightful, safe and friendly setting for young children to stroke and feed a range of familiar animals. The Williamson's Family Fair is an added attraction, rides individually priced (seasonal opening 11am-5pm). Open daily, 10am-5pm. Closed 25th, 26th Dec and 1st Jan. (See also "Free Places" chapter.) 01603 783762.
Schools
Open all year

C2 (D) **Amazonia World of Reptiles,** Central Seafront, Marine Parade, **Great Yarmouth.** Set in the midst of botanical gardens is Britain's largest collection of reptiles, from snakes and lizards to crocodilians. Open daily, Mar-Oct, 10am-5pm (7pm in Summer). 01493 842202.
Schools

(F) **Berney Marshes,** RSPB, 4 miles W of **Great Yarmouth.** See "Free Places" chapter.

(B) **Fairhaven Woodland and Water Garden,** School Road, **South Walsham.** Over three miles of walks through beautiful ancient woodland, which boasts a 950-year-old King Oak, with views, children's trail and boat trips across South Walsham Inner Broad. Nature reserve with bird hide Open daily, 10am-5pm; May-Aug, 9pm, Wed and Thurs; closed 25th Dec. 01603 270449. www.norfolkbroads.com/fairhaven
Schools
Open all year

Price Codes for a family of four: (A): less than £5 (B): £5-£10 (C): £10-£15 (D): £15-£20 (E): £20-£30 (G): £30-£50 (H): Over £50 (F): Free
Map Ref: Grid square on Page 2 Map   Schools: Facilities available   ● Birthday parties

MAP REFS	PRICE CODES
C2	

Fritton Lake Countryworld, on A143, near **Great Yarmouth,** has 250 acres of countryside beside one of the most beautiful lakes in East Anglia. Attractions include Falconry Centre, heavy horse stables, cart rides, Friends Farm, an adventure playground and boating on the lake. Special events held throughout Summer. Open daily Easter-end Sept, 10am-5.30pm. 01493 488288/488208.
(D) Schools

The Otter Trust, Earsham, off A143, near Bungay. An otter sanctuary where you can also see a variety of wildfowl and muntjac deer. Riverside walks, three lakes, an adventure playground for small children, tearoom and gift shop make for a good day out. Open daily, Apr-30th Oct, 10.30am-6pm. 01986 893470.
(D) Schools

Pets Corner, Oulton Broads, **Lowestoft,** is a lovely children's petting farm located on the edge of Nicholas Everitt Park. There are lots of animals for children to see including chickens, ducks, geese, rabbits, monkeys, snakes, ponies, parrots and owls. Open daily, 23rd Mar-1st week Nov, 10am-5pm. 01502 563533.
(B)

Pettitts Animal Adventure Park, Reedham, off A47 between Norwich and Great Yarmouth, is a delight for younger children. Attractively landscaped, the park offers hours of fun with shows, animals, a miniature railway, tiny-tot roller coaster and vintage toy-car ride. Refreshments available. Open daily 16th Mar-27th Oct, 10.30am-5pm (5.30pm during Summer). 01493 700094.
(E) Schools

Redwings Horse Sanctuary, Caldecott Hall Visitor Centre, **Fritton,** 1 mile NE of Fritton on A143 Gt Yarmouth to Beccles road. Meet the rescued horses, ponies and donkeys and watch the horse-handling demonstrations. Stroll along the paddock walks and 'adopt' a rescued animal. Information centre and gift shop. Open 10am-5pm, daily, 24th Mar-8th Apr; Sun and Mon, 14th Apr-15th Jul; daily, 20th Jul-2nd Sept; Sun and Mon, 8th Sept-28th Oct. 01493 488531. www.redwings.co.uk
(B) Schools

Sea Life Centre, Marine Parade, **Great Yarmouth.** Submerge yourself into the secret world of the sea-bed, and have close encounters with all manner of under-water creatures. Meet sharks and rays, shrimps and seahorses and enjoy the feeding displays, demonstrations and talks. Learn how you can help with marine conservation. Open daily, from 10am; closed 25th Dec. 01493 330631. www.sealife.co.uk
(D) Schools Open all year

Strumpshaw Fen, RSPB, Staithe Cottage, Low Road, **Strumpshaw.** Wetland with 6 miles of trails through reedbeds, wet meadows, grazing marshes, rivers and dykes. Rich in bird, insect and plant life. Open daily, dawn-dusk; closed 25th Dec. 01603 715191. www.rspb.org.uk
(B) Open all year

Suffolk Wildlife Park, Kessingland, off A12 near Lowestoft, is the place to see a collection of African wildlife including lions, cheetahs, giraffes and chimpanzees. For the less energetic you can view the park in style on a safari road train. There is also a play area, indoor amusement centre, gift shop and restaurant. Open daily, 10am-5pm (4pm in Winter). Closed 25th-26th Dec. 01502 740291. www.suffolkwildlifepark.co.uk
(E) Schools Open all year

Thrigby Hall Wildlife Gardens, Filby, near Great Yarmouth. The grounds of Thrigby Hall are home to a surprising selection of wild and exotic beasts. From Sumatran Tigers and Red Pandas to crocodiles, reptiles, monkeys and more, offering an exciting day out for the family. Picnic at leisure while the children go wild in the adventure play area. Open daily, 10am-5.30pm, or dusk if earlier. 01493 369477. www.optipoint.co.uk/thrigby
(D) Schools Open all year

Village Experience, Burgh St Margaret, Fleggburgh, offers family fun for all ages, from tots to grandparents. From traditional fairground rides, farm animals, and train rides to classic vehicles, bygones and memorabilia. Indoor themed play area. Ring or visit website for opening times. 01493 369770. www.thevillage-experience.com
(D) Schools

Price Codes for a family of four: (A): less than £5 (B): £5-£10 (C): £10-£15 (D): £15-£20 (E): £20-£30 (G): £30-£50 (H): Over £50 (F): Free
Map Ref: Grid square on Page 2 Map   Schools: Facilities available   ● Birthday parties

Farms, Wildlife & Nature Parks

MAP REFS	PRICE CODES		
C3	Tour Ⓑ Open all year	**Bruiseyard Vineyard, Winery and Herb Centre**, near Saxmundham. Explore the 10 acre vineyard with 40 minute audio tour followed by a video and wine tasting for the adults. You can enjoy wandering in the herb and water gardens and the children will love the play area. Picnic area and restaurant. Open Tues-Sun, 10.30am-5pm. Closed 25th Dec-15th Jan. 01728 638281.	
	Ⓕ Schools Open all year	**Dunwich Heath and Minsmere Beach**, NT, Saxmundham. See "Free Places" chapter.	
	Ⓓ Schools 🎈	**Easton Farm Park**, Easton, near Wickham Market, Woodbridge, was voted Suffolk Family Attraction of the Year, 2001. There are lots of farm animals, including Suffolk Punch horses. Watch the cows being milked, touch and feed the animals, 'pat-a-pet', and free pony rides, daily (ring for times). Visit the new indoor soft play area and battery operated tractors. Open daily, 23rd Mar-29th Sept, 10.30am-6pm, and daily, Feb and Oct Half Term Hols. 10.30am-4pm. 01728 746475. www.eastonfarmpark.co.uk (See Advert page 66.)	
	Ⓕ Schools Open all year	**Foxburrow Farm**, Saddlemakers Lane, **Melton**. See "Free Places" chapter.	
	Ⓕ Schools Open all year	**Landguard Point**, Viewpoint Rd, **Felixstowe**. See "Free Places" chapter.	
	Ⓑ Schools Open all year	**Minsmere Nature Reserve**, near Dunwich, signposted from Westleton, is a premier RSPB site containing 2000 acres of varied heathland, marsh, reedbed and woodlands. Facilities include hides, nature trails, tearoom and shop. Adjacent Dunwich Heath. Open daily, except Tues, 9am-9pm (or sunset if earlier). Members Ⓕ. 01728 648281.	
	Ⓕ Schools Open all year 🎈	**Valley Farm White Animal Collection**, **Wickham Market**. See "Free Places" chapter.	

Mole Hall
Wildlife Park & Butterfly Pavilion

The Otters Are Waiting To See You

Gift Shop / Wild Flowers & Herbs

A Great Day Out

To Cambridge — To Saffron Walen
B1383 — Newport — To Thaxted
Quendon — Ugley — Mole Hall
Stansted B1383 — Widdington

Many Species Of Animals & Birds
Pets Corner / Play Area
Cafe / Picnic Area
Saffron Walden 01799 540400

OLD MACDONALDS educational FARM PARK

Where the Countryside comes to life

Open all year
except
Christmas and Boxing Day
10am - 6pm or dusk

Weald Road,
South Weald,
Brentwood,
Essex CM14 5AY

Tel **(01277) 375177**

SPEND A DAY IN THE COUNTRY AT
EASTON FARM PARK

Farm Animals • Suffolk Horses
Dairy Centre • Pets Paddocks
Green Trail • Gift Shop
Picnic Area • Tearoom • Facepainting
'Pat-a-Pet' & Free Pony Rides daily
(ring for times)
Childrens Battery Operated Tractors
New Indoor Soft Play Area

Open Daily 10.30am - 6.00pm 23rd March - 29th September
Open Daily Feb & October Half Terms - Half Price
(10.30am-4pm)

SIGNPOSTED OFF THE A12
Easton Nr. Wickham Market, Suffolk
Telephone: (01728) 746475
www.eastonfarmpark.co.uk

Theme Parks & Play Parks

(See also "Play Centres" in the Directory).

MAP REFS | **PRICE CODES**

A1 — Ⓑ **Jungle Wonderland,** The First Floor, Pier Entertainment Centre, The Green, Open all year — Hunstanton. Patrolled by rangers, the centre caters for children from 2-12 years and 🎈 under 1.5m, with soft play area, aerial walkways, giant ball pool, tunnels, Kenny the Croc slide and 80-seater diner. Open daily Apr-Oct, 10am-6pm; weekends and school hols only, Nov-Mar, 10am-6pm. 01485 535505.

A3 — Ⓐ **Kid's Kingdom at Laserquest,** 2nd Floor, 13-15 Bradwells Court, **Cambridge,** is Open all year an indoor adventure play area for the under 7s featuring a bouncy castle and ball pond. 🎈 Open daily 10.30am-9pm. Closed 24th-26th Dec, 1st Jan. 01223 302102.

Ⓑ **Rascals,** Stansted Road, **Bishop's Stortford,** a large multi-level indoor play centre for Open all year 5-12 year olds. Separate toddler area, bouncy castle and café. Open daily 10am-6.30pm, 🎈 Mon, 12 o'clock opening, closed Christmas. 01279 755771.

A4 — Ⓑ **Adventure Island Playbarn,** Parsonage Lane, **Sawbridgeworth.** This indoor Open all year softplay centre has lots of features including a ball pond and aerial runway. There is a 🎈 separate area for toddlers. The outdoor picnic area has a bouncy castle and play equipment. Height restriction 1.5m. Open 10am-6pm. Closed 24th-27th Dec, 1st Jan. 01279 600907.

Ⓑ **Als Adventure World,** Fairlop Waters Country Park, near **Ilford,** is a three level Open all year indoor adventure playground for children from 4-12 years and 'Jungle Babes' for under 4s. 🎈 Open daily, 10am-7pm. Closed 25th-26th Dec, 1st Jan. 020 8500 9922.

🎈 Ⓑ **Chuckle City,** Festival Leisure Park, **Basildon,** offers a fantastic adventure area for Schools children aged 0-11. Babes in arms are free and there is a Chuckles Diner on site. Open Open all year daily, 10.30am-6.30pm. Closed 25th, 26th Dec, 1st Jan. 01268 531525.

Ⓑ Schools **Hobbs Cross Open Farm,** Theydon Garnon, near Epping, has an adventure Open all year playbarn featuring soft play apparatus and a toddlers room. 01992 814764. (See also 🎈 "Farms" chapter.)

🎈 Ⓑ **Kids Kingdom,** Wood Lane Sports Centre, **Dagenham,** is a large multi-level indoor play Schools centre with slides, ball pools and aerial runways. There is a separate toddler area with Open all year bouncy castle and a café. Open daily, 10am-6pm. Closed 24th-27th Dec. 020 8984 8828.

Ⓑ **Kids Korner,** Epping New Road, **Epping,** is a large multi-level indoor play centre Schools offering a range of activities including three slides, ball pools and a climbing wall. There Open all year is a separate toddler area and a café where you can enjoy both hot and cold food. Open 🎈 daily, 10am-6.30pm, (last admission 5pm) 01992 813413.

Ⓑ **Pirates,** Latton Bush, **Harlow,** is a children's indoor adventure playground featuring Open all year soft play apparatus, including ball ponds, slides and cargo nets. Separate well equipped play 🎈 area for the under 5s. Open daily, 10am-5.30pm. Closed Mons in term-time. 01279 422400.

Ⓑ **Sprogg.com,** Lakeside, **Thurrock,** offers supervised play for 2-8 year olds in a Open all year wonderful, stimulating environment, including motorised ride-ons, computer games, 🎈 ballpool, slide and soft-play area, cartoon cinema, library, toys and games etc. Parent and Toddler sessions Mon-Fri, 10am-3pm. Open daily 10am-6pm Mon-Fri, 9am-6pm Sat, 11am-5pm. Sun. Closed 25th-26th Dec. 01708 890864. www.sprogg.com

---

Price Codes for a family of four: Ⓐ: less than £5 Ⓑ: £5-£10 Ⓒ: £10-£15 Ⓓ: £15-£20 Ⓔ: £20-£30 Ⓖ: £30-£50 Ⓗ: Over £50 Ⓕ: Free
Map Ref: Grid square on Page 2 Map   Schools: Facilities available   🎈 Birthday parties

MAP REFS	PRICE CODES

B1 — Ⓑ Schools, Open all year — **Funstop,** Exchange House, Louden Road, **Cromer.** The giant slide, tubes, scramble nets, ball pond and under-3s fun play area offers fun for toddlers to 10 year olds. Under 3s pay less. Open 10am-6pm, May-Sept, daily; Oct-Apr, open Fri, Sat, Sun and school hols, closed 25th/26th Dec. 01263 514976.

Ⓑ Schools — **Playland,** Wells-next-the-Sea, next to the picturesque harbour and Quay. Children's indoor fun house, with a soft play area for toddlers. Open weekends and school hols, 10am-5pm. 01328 711656.

B2 — Ⓔ Schools — **Dinosaur Adventure Park,** Weston Park, **Lenwade,** is 9 miles from Norwich, off the A1067 Fakenham Road. Something for all age groups: dinosaur trail, woodland maze, adventure play areas, deer safari, jurassic putt crazy golf, raptor races, education centre, secret animal garden with petting barns, clim-a-saurus. Open 10am-5pm, Fri-Sun, 23rd Mar-8th Apr; daily, 9th Apr-9th Sept; Fri-Sun, 10th-21st Sept; daily, 22nd-28th Oct. 01603 870245. www.dinosaurpark.co.uk

Ⓑ Schools, Open all year — **Playbarn,** West Green Farm, Shotesham Road, **Poringland.** This indoor play centre, for the under 7s, is based on a farmyard theme. The courtyard is filled with pedal tractors and outdoor toys. There is a tiny tots soft play area and reading and puzzle tables for all-weather play. Open Mon-Fri, 9.30am-3.30pm, Sun 10am-5pm. Barn Farm opens to the public Easter-Oct, with individually-priced pony rides, farm tours, tractor and trailer rides. Closed 25th-26th Dec and 1st Jan. 01508 495526. www.playbarn.co.uk

B3 — Ⓑ Open all year — **Activity World,** Station Hill, **Bury St Edmunds.** Lots of fun for children under 1.5m tall, with slides, flumes, ball pools, rope bridges a vertical drop slide and trampoline. There is a separate two level area for under 5s and a fast food diner for refreshments. Children can also join the Breakfast, After-School or Holiday Clubs, and for toddlers there is the Panda Club. Open daily, 9.30am-6.30pm. 01284 763799. www.activityworld.co.uk (See Advert page 71.)

Ⓑ Open all year — **Go Bananas,** The Cowdray Centre, **Colchester,** is a fantastic three level "Jungle Adventure" play centre including climbing wall and space ball ride. There is a separate "Tiny Town" for under 5s and a Bananas Cafe for parents. Open daily, 9.30am-6.30pm. Closed 25th, 26th Dec, 1st Jan & Easter Sun. 01206 761762.

Ⓑ Open all year — **Jim's Totally Brilliant Play Ltd,** Whitehouse Road, **Ipswich,** is a huge indoor play complex. "Nurseryland" for 4s and under. Megazone for 7s and over. Open Tues-Sun, 10am-7pm. Closed Christmas. 01473 464616.

Ⓑ Schools, Open all year — **Kabookees,** 1 Addison Rd, **Sudbury,** is a multi-level indoor adventure playground with slides, ballpools and aerial runway. Separate toddler area. Day nursery and creche are available (phone for details) and the restaurant has delicious home-cooked food. Open daily, 10am-6pm. Closed 25th/26th Dec. 01787 311163. kabookees@ianrober.globalnet.co.uk

Ⓑ Schools, Open all year — **The Ultimate Kid'z Kingdom,** Gloster Rd, **Martlesham Heath.** Huge 3 level indoor adventure play area, cargo nets, slides, jungle run and jungle race way, bouncy castle etc. Separate toddler playzone. Open daily 9.30am-6.30pm. Closed 25th-26th Dec. 01473 611333/611111.

Ⓑ — **Playworld,** at Mid Suffolk Leisure Centre, **Stowmarket,** is a multi-activity adventure playground. Whizz around in a racing car on the Grand Prix course or have a spin in a "Dizzy Dodger"! Open end Apr-end Sept, daily 9.30am-7pm; weekends 9am-6pm. 01449 742817.

B4 — Ⓖ Schools — **Adventure Island,** next to **Southend Pier,** is a traditional amusement park plus a new all-water theme park with slides and flumes. Open Easter-mid Sept, daily, 11am-10pm; weekends in Winter and school hols 11am-6pm. Special events may continue later. 01702 468023. www.adventureisland.co.uk

---

Price Codes for a family of four: Ⓐ: less than £5 Ⓑ: £5-£10 Ⓒ: £10-£15 Ⓓ: £15-£20 Ⓔ: £20-£30 Ⓖ: £30-£50 Ⓗ: Over £50 Ⓕ: Free
Map Ref: Grid square on Page 2 Map   Schools: Facilities available   ● Birthday parties

Theme Parks & Play Parks

MAP REFS	PRICE CODES		
B4	Open all year		**Clacton Pier,** is a traditional seaside pier with all the attractions of the Fairground. With free entry you can stroll along the pier and use the free deck chairs to sit back and enjoy the sea air. Open daily in high season, selected rides other times. 01255 421115.
	Schools Open all year	Ⓑ 🎈	**Kids Kingdom,** Garon Park, Eastern Ave., **Southend,** is an enormous indoor play centre offering a range of exciting play activities plus outdoor play equipment, a garden and a barbecue in Summer. Height restriction 1.5m or age 12 whichever comes first. Open daily 10am-6pm. Closed 24th-27th Dec. 01702 462747.
	Open all year	Ⓑ 🎈	**Rascals,** Gorse Lane Industrial Estate, **Clacton-on-Sea,** a large multi-level indoor play centre for 5-12 year olds. Separate toddler area and café. Open daily, 10am-6.30pm, Mon, 12 o'clock opening. Closed Christmas. 01255 475755.
		Ⓕ	**Southend Pier.** See "Free Places" chapter.
C1	Open all year	Ⓑ 🎈	**Elephant Playbarn,** Mundesley Road, **Knapton**. For children aged 1-8, this converted flint barn is full of soft play toys, ball pools, bouncy castles and climbing frames. There are weekly music classes and a second-hand clothes club. Open Wed-Fri, 10am-4pm, Sat and Sun, 10am-5pm; daily during school hols, 10am-4pm; closed for 2 weeks at Christmas. 01263 721080.
C2	Open all year	Ⓑ 🎈	**East Point Pavilion Visitors' Centre,** Royal Plain, **Lowestoft,** has "Mayhem", an indoor soft play platform for children up to 12 years. Open daily, Apr-Sept, 9.30am-5.30pm; Oct-Mar, Mon-Fri, 10.30am-5pm, Sat-Sun, 10am-5pm. 01502 533600.
			Joyland, Marine Parade, **Great Yarmouth,** gives children all the fun of the fair, with rides including Snails, Tubs and Pirate Ship and a Toy Town Mountain with kiddies' rollercoaster. Open Easter-Oct. 01493 844094.
		Ⓑ	**Louis Tussaud's House of Wax,** 18 Regent Road, **Great Yarmouth,** includes many famous personalities, torture chambers, a chamber of horrors, a hall of funny mirrors and family amusement arcade. Open Easter-Oct.
		Ⓑ	**Merrivale Model Village,** Marine Parade, **Great Yarmouth.** Fantasy-land of town and countryside in miniature. Over 200 models include a working fairground, gypsy encampment, farm, filling station and railway. Illuminated at dusk during Summer season. Open daily, Easter-31st May, 9.30am-5.30pm; Jun-Oct, 10am-10pm. 01493 842097.
	Schools	Ⓖ	**Pleasure Beach,** South Beach Parade, **Great Yarmouth.** This 9-acre seafront amusement park features over 70 rides and attractions. There are thrills, fun and terror to be had on the many rides from Terminator, White Knuckle, Twister, Log Flume and Yo Yo Safari train to ghost trains, go-karts, monorail and galloping horses. Open Mar-Oct. Please phone for opening times as these vary. 01493 844585.
		Ⓖ 🎈	**Pleasurewood Hills,** Leisure Way, between **Great Yarmouth** and **Lowestoft** offers over 50 rides, shows and attractions. Pay once at the gate for action all day long (min. height requirement for some rides). Open Easter and Bank Hol weekends, daily in Summer season, selected weekends in Autumn. 01502 586000. www.pleasurewoodhills.co.uk
C3			**Charles Manning's Amusement Park,** Sea Road, **Felixstowe,** provides seaside amusements. Admission based on tokens. Open Easter-end Sept, weekends and school holidays. 01394 282370.
	Open all year		**Felixstowe Pier,** has rides, amusements and sideshows. 01394 284680.
	Schools Open all year	🎈	**Walton Pier, Walton-on-the-Naze.** Rides suitable for younger children include tea-cups, roundabouts, bikes and cars, whilst older ones can experience the thrills of the waltzer, gallopers, flying coaster and more. (See also "Directory" and "Trips" chapters.) 01255 672288.

Price Codes for a family of four: Ⓐ: less than £5 Ⓑ: £5-£10 Ⓒ: £10-£15 Ⓓ: £15-£20 Ⓔ: £20-£30 Ⓖ: £30-£50 Ⓗ: Over £50 Ⓕ: Free
Map Ref: Grid square on Page 2 Map Schools: Facilities available 🎈 Birthday parties

FIRST FOR FAMILIES!

PARADISE
WILDLIFE PARK
BROXBOURNE, HERTS

NEW Shows For 2002
- The Hollywood Stunt Parrots
- Reptile Mania

PLUS...
- Klondyke Krazy Golf
- Meet Safari Sam Daily

NEW Opening Hours 9.30am to 6.00pm

NEW FOR 2002... Wonderful World Of Reptiles!

See The Lions!

World's Largest Inflatable Paddling Pool!

Meet Safari Sam

Children (2-15) **£6.50**
Adults **£8.50** Senior Citizens **£6.50**
Paradise Wildlife Park
White Stubbs Lane, Broxbourne, Herts EN10 7QA
Just off the **A10** at **Broxbourne**
Signposted from **Junction 25** on the **M25**
Tel: 01992-470490 • www.pwpark.com

ONE CHILD FREE WITH TWO PAYING ADULTS
Valid until 31st December 2002. Cannot be used in conjunction with any other offer.
NOT VALID ON BANK HOLIDAYS. LETS GO

See Our New **EVEN BIGGER** Website For Discounts & Promotions

www.pwpark.com
The Web's Favourite Wildlife Park!

Places to Go Outside the Area

HERTFORDSHIRE

Paradise Wildlife Park, Broxbourne, is a truly special place with a relaxed and friendly atmosphere. The Park has an excellent range of animals including tigers, lions, red pandas, cheetahs, birds of prey, reptiles, monkeys, zebra, camels and reindeer. What makes it unique is the fact that you can get really close, meeting and feeding the animals. It is conveniently located just off the A10 and only 6 miles from Jn 25 of the M25. A courtesy mini-bus service operates from Broxbourne main line station, which has direct links to London and Cambridge. The park offers many other attractions including children's rides, three themed adventure playgrounds, woodland walk, tractor trailer rides and an indoor soft play area for under 5s. See the Hollywood Stunts Parrot show and the Big Bug show, all of which are included in the admission price. There is a small charge for the Woodland Railway and Pony Rides. There is a good range of catering outlets and ample picnic areas are located around the Park. Open daily, Mar-Oct, 9.30am-6pm, Nov-Feb, 10am-dusk. 01992 470490. www.pwpark.com (See Advert page 70.)

Schools Open all year

SUSSEX

Cambridge Language & Activity Courses, CLAC, organises interesting Summer courses for 8-13 year and 14-17 year olds at two separate sites in lovely countryside locations, Lavant House and Slindon College, West Sussex. The idea is to bring together British and foreign students to create natural language exchange in a motivated and fun environment. There are French, German and Spanish classes for British students and English for overseas students. Fully supervised in a safe environment, there are lots of activities such as swimming, tennis, team games and competitions, drama and music, in addition to the language tuition. Residential or not, these courses offer enjoyable multi-activity weeks with 20 hours of specific tuition in small groups. Courses run weekly during July and August. For more details and a brochure call 01223 846348. www.clac.org.uk (See Advert centre section.)

Turn that frown upside down play at the wackiest place in town

Visit Britains Most Exciting Indoor Adventure Playgrounds

For further details of Birthday Parties
Out of School Childcare
Play Centre opening times and prices

Activity World & Toddler World
Bury St Edmunds

Telephone
01284 763799
or visit
www.activityworld.co.uk

PLACES TO GO - ALL OVER THE COUNTRY

LOG ONTO
www.letsgowiththechildren.co.uk

Index

Abbey Visitors' Centre at Samson's Tower	51
Activity World	68, 71
Ada Cole Memorial Stables	59
Adventure Activities	13
Amazonia World of Reptiles	63
Ancient House Museum	49
Anglesey Abbey	46
Anglo-Saxon Village	51
Anville Falconry	57
Audley End House and Park	46
Banham Zoo	61
Barleylands Farm and Museum	47, 60
Basildon Zoo	60
Baylham House Rare Breeds Farm	62
Berney Arms Windmill	55
Bicycle Hire	13
Bircham Windmill	45
Bishop Bonner's Cottages Museum	7
Blicking Hall	47
Boat Hire	13
Boat Trips	26
Botanic Gardens	49
Bourne Mill	51
Bowling (Ten Pin)	14
Boydell's Farm	57
Bradwell Nuclear Power Station	9
Braintree Museum	46
Brancaster Millennium Activity Centre	60
Brass Rubbing	14
Brentwood Centre	19, 20
Bressingham Steam Experience & Gardens	49
Bridewell Museum	49
Broads Authority	24
Bruiseyard Vineyard	65
Burston Strike School	7
Buying Furniture	14, 28
Caister Castle Car Collection	55
Caister St Edmund	55
Cambridge Language & Activity Courses	71
Cambridge Museum & Attractions	3, 46
Castle Acre Priory & Castle	49
Castle Point Transport Museum	54
Castle Rising Castle	45
Central Museum Planetarium	54
Central Trains	27
Chelmsford Museum	5
Cinemas	14
Cley Marshes	60
Coggeshall Grange Barn	51
Colchester Castle	51
Colchester Zoo	62
Collectors World & The Magical Dickens Experience	45
Colne Valley Railway	51
Country & Nature Parks	3
Crazy Golf	15
Cromer Lifeboat & Museum	6
Cromer Museum	48
Dedham Art & Craft Centre and Toy Museum	8
Denver Windmill	45
Dunwich Underwater Exploration Exhibition	55
East Anglia Transport Museum	55
East Anglian Railway Museum	52
East Essex Aviation Society Museum	10
Easton Farm Park	65, 66
EcoTech	49
Elizabethan House Museum	55
Essex Secret Bunker	52
Fairhaven Woodland and Water Garden	63
Felbrigg Hall	48
Forncett Industrial Steam Museum	50
Fowlmere Nature Reserve	57
Framlingham Castle	56
Free Places	3
Fritton Lake Countryworld	64
Gainsborough's House	7
Gifford's Hall Vineyard	62
Gosfield Hall	52
Green Quay	57
Grimes Caves	50
Guildhall of Corpus Christi	53
Happisburgh Lighthouse	54
Harlow Attractions	7
Harwich Lifeboat Museum	52
Harwich Maritime Museum	52
Harwich Redoubt Fort	52
Hayes Hill Farm & Holyfield Hall Farm	60
Hedingham Castle	52
Hickling Broad Nature Reserve	63
Hillside Animal Sanctuary	61
Hobbs Cross Open Farm	60
Holkham Hall	48
Horsey Windpump	54
Houghton Hall	48
House on the Hill Adventure	46
Hunstanton Sea Life & Marine Sanctuary	57
Ice Skating	15
Iceni Village and Museums	50
Ickworth	46
Imperial War Museum Duxford	46
Inspire Hands-On Science Centre	50
Ipswich Borough Council Facilities	17, 19, 22, 24
Ipswich Transport Museum	52
Jakapeni Rare Breeds Farm	62
Karting	16
Kentwell Hall	53
King's Lynn Museums	48
Langham Glass	11
Laser Fun	16
Layer Marney Tower	62
Lee Valley Information Centre	5
Letheringsett Watermill	48
Linton Zoo	59
Little Hall	53
Local Councils	16
London Attractions	29
Long Shop Museum	56
Lowestoft and East Suffolk Maritime Museum	55
Maize Maze	16
Mangapps Farm Railway Museum	54
Mannington Gardens & Countryside	60
Manor House Museum	53
Maritime Museum	55
Marks Hall Estate & Arboretum	62
Marsh Farm	60
Mechanical Music Museum and Bygones	53
Melford Hall	63
Minsmere Nature Reserve	65
Mistley Park Animal Rescue and Environmental Centre	62
Mole Hall Wildlife Park	59, 65
Mountfitchet Castle and Norman Village	46
Muckleburgh Collection	48
Museum of East Anglian Life	53
Museum of the Broads	56
Music & Movement	16
Mustard Shop	50
National Horseracing Museum	46, 5
National Motor Boat Museum	5
Norfolk Lavender	5
Norfolk Motor Cycle Museum	5
Norfolk Nelson Museum	5
Norfolk Shire Horse Centre	5
Norfolk Wildlife Centre and Country Park	6
Northey Island	1
Norwich Attractions	4
Norwich Puppet Theatre	2
Old MacDonalds Educational Farm Park	60, 6
100th Bomb Group Museum	5
Orford Castle	5
Origins - The History Mix	5
Otter Trust	6
Oxburgh Hall	4
Pakenham Water Mill	5
Paradise Park	70, 7
Park Farm	5
Paycockes	5
Pensthorpe Waterfowl Park	6
Pets Corner	6
Pettitts Animal Adventure Park	6
Pier Museum	5
Pitch and Putt	1
Play Centres	6
Pleasurewood Hills	6
Pottery Painting	6
Pottery Workshops	6
Putting Greens	1
RAF Air Defence Radar Museum	5
Raptor Foundation	6
Redwings Horse Sanctuary	6
Roller Skating, Boarding & BMX	1
Roots of Norfolk at Gressenhall - Norfolk Rural Life Museum	50, 6
Row 111 Houses/Old Merchant's House	5
Royal Norfolk Regimental Museum	5
Saffron Walden Museum	5
Sainsbury Centre for Visual Arts	5
Sandringham	4
Saxstead Green Post Mill	5
Sea Life Adventure	5
Sea Life Centre	5
Secret Nuclear Bunker	5
Shell Museum	6
Shepreth Wildlife Park	58
Sheringham Museum	5
Shirehall (Courthouse) Museum	5
Snow Sports	1
Somerleyton Hall and Gardens	5
Southend Attractions	6
Spectator Sports	18
Spedeworth International	18
Sports & Leisure Centres	1
Strangers' Hall	5
Strumpshaw Fen	6
Strumpshaw Steam Museum	5
Suffolk Horse Museum	5
Suffolk Owl Sanctuary	6
Suffolk Wildlife Park	6
Sutton Windmill and Broads Museum	5
Swaffham Museum	5
Swimming Pools	21
Theatres	2
Theme Parks & Play Parks	6
Thrigby Hall Wildlife Gardens	6
Thursford Collection	5
Tilbury Fort	5
Tollhouse Museum	5
Tots to Teens Furniture	14
Tourist Information Centres	2
Train Trips	2
Tropical Butterfly World	6
Valley Farm White Animal Collection	6
Village Experience	5
Walton Hall Farm Museum	5
Water Fun Parks	2
Watersports	2
Wells & Walsingham Light Railway	27
Wells Maritime Museum	5
Wildfowl and Wetlands Trust	5
Wimpole Hall	4
Wimpole Home Farm	6
Wingfield College and Gardens	5
Wolferton Hall and Park	5
Woodbridge Museum	5
Woodbridge Tide Mill	5
Wroxham Barns	5
Wymondham Heritage Museum	5